Ardent love to Jesus

The reverse of 1842 Jubilee Medal struck in commemoration
of the 50th anniversary of the Baptist Missionary Society

Ardent love to Jesus

English Baptists
and the experience of revival
in the long eighteenth century

Michael A. G. Haykin

BRYNTIRION PRESS

First published 2013

ISBN: 978 1 85049 248 1

Evangelical Movement of Wales

The EMW works in both Welsh and English and seeks to help Christians and churches by:
• running children's camps and family conferences
• providing theological training and events for ministers
• running Christian bookshops and a conference centre
• publishing magazines and books

Bryntirion Press is a ministry of EMW

Past issues of EMW magazines and sermons preached at our conferences are available on our web site: www.emw.org.uk

Published by Bryntirion Press, Bryntirion, Bridgend CF31 4DX, Wales, in association with EP BOOKS, Faverdale North, Darlington, DL3 0PH, UK.

EP BOOKS are distributed in the USA by: JPL Fulfillment, 3741 Linden Avenue Southeast, Grand Rapids, MI 49548.
E-mail: sales@jplfulfillment.com
Tel: 877.683.6935

For my dear children,
two of the most precious joys in my life,
my daughter Victoria and my son Nigel

Contents

Acknowledgements

I vividly recall in the mid-1980s, in the library of what was then Central Baptist Seminary on Jonesville Avenue in North York, Toronto, taking down the third volume of the standard American edition of Andrew Fuller's works from one of the shelves, and beginning to read Fuller's circular letter *The Promise of the Spirit, the Grand Encouragement in Promoting the Gospel*. Little did I know it at the time but I was hooked — hooked on Fuller and his friends! In time, this led to my writing, among other things, a major biography of Fuller's close friend John Sutcliff — *One heart and one soul: John Sutcliff of Olney, his friends, and his times* (Evangelical Press, 1994) — various papers on Fuller and his circle, a study of Fuller's piety, *The Armies of the Lamb: The spirituality of Andrew Fuller* (Joshua Press, 2001), and initiating the Andrew Fuller Works Project that is seeking to publish critical editions of all of Fuller's works. The intertwined thought and lives of this 'band of brothers', truly perichoretic because of their being indwelt by the same Spirit of the Lord Jesus, has deeply ministered to me, though they have been in glory now for nearly two centuries. This small book encapsulates some of my experience of listening to these friends, and seeking to find from their walk with Christ wisdom for living in these days.

The immediate impetus for this book was the invitation to deliver a series of talks at the 2010 Revival Conference of the Wales Evangelical School of Theology, Bryntirion, Bridgend, in South Wales from 4-9 July. I am deeply thankful to Dr Jonathan Stephen, Dr Eryl Davies, and Mr Kerry Orchard for this privilege, and also to Dr Davies for accepting this manuscript for publication. It was with profound Christian joy that I gave these talks at that conference, enjoying fellowship with these brothers as well as the other brothers and sisters who attended the conference. It was while I was preparing these talks that I saw the material could be put together easily as a small book. Where some of this material has appeared before in print, I have made specific acknowledgement. But much of the material has also been given as lectures over the past twenty years in various contexts in North America and the British Isles. Although no specific acknowledgement is made in this case, I am deeply appreciative of the many invitations from churches and seminaries to speak on this material, and also for the feedback that I have received.

One of the chapters, chapter 3, which deals with friendship and revival, was suggested to me as a result of giving the Radical Reformation Day Lecture at Southwestern Baptist Theological Seminary on 20 January 2011. I am indebted to Dr Paige Patterson, the President of Southwestern, for the invitation to give that lecture, and for the warm Texan hospitality I experienced on the occasion.

To the Triune God, the best and the greatest, be glory!

Michael A.G. Haykin
Dundas, Ontario
2011 — the 250th anniversary
of the birth of William Carey

Introduction

The passing of the Act of Uniformity by the English Parliament on 24 August 1662, which required ministers to adhere fully to all of the detail of worship laid out in the *Book of Common Prayer*, led to upwards of two thousand Anglican pastors, denominated by history as Puritans and, in many ways, the spiritual heart of the established church, leaving their parishes and manses for the sake of conscience. These Puritan leaders and the various communities in which they subsequently found themselves — known also as Dissenters or Nonconformists and subdivided into three major groups, the Presbyterians, Congregationalists and Particular Baptists — were subsequently subject to 'calculated and often malicious persecution' over the next twenty-six years.[1] Despite this persecution, however, these various Puritan bodies thrived and even grew in numbers.

In 1685, the monarch who had been reigning through much of this persecution, Charles II, died and was succeeded by his brother who became James II. James was a Roman Catholic and reigned but three years. The Anglican leaders around him began to fear that James would lead England back under the tyranny of Rome. They thus engineered a coup that would oust James and place James' son-in-law, the Dutch prince William of Orange, on the throne as William III.[2] This revolution, sometimes described as the Glorious Revolution, meant the dawn of a new era for those Christian communities outside of the Church of England. In 1689 William III authorized the passing of the Act of Toleration, which gave the Dissenters freedom of worship and immunity from persecution, although certain civil restrictions against them remained in force. There is little doubt that, as G. M. Ditchfield puts it, the accession of William III, with his wife, Mary II, occasioned 'a fundamental change of ecclesiastical régime'.[3]

One would expect that with such freedom Puritan Dissent would flourish. But, in fact, a large degree of stagnation and even decline set in. The Presbyterians began to be submerged by the growing rationalism of the day, eventually being unable to prevent serious doubts about the doctrine of the Trinity and the deity of Christ springing up amongst them like noxious weeds. By the early 1730s they were in sad decline and would become extinct as an evangelical denomination by the end of the eighteenth century. The Baptist John Ryland Jr (1753–1825) described them seventy or so years later in 1816 as 'almost universally Socinianized', that is, totally given over to Unitarianism.[4]

The Congregationalists and the Particular Baptists, on the other hand, maintained a distinct commitment to the main lines of Christian orthodoxy but became increasingly insular as the years wore on. Far too many of them retreated within the four walls of their meeting-houses, fostered an introspective piety and spurned evangelism — some of them on the basis of a Hyper-Calvinism that denied true moral agency. Due to a deep-seated prejudice against the state church, understandable in light of their history in the seventeenth century, there was a distinct inability to discern God's hand at work in the Calvinistic Methodist revivals of their day. Unlike the Presbyterians, however, revival would come to their ranks in the latter half of the eighteenth century, and that, in part, because of their tenacious hold on classic Christianity. By the first decade of the next century, the low-burning embers in their churches had been fanned into white-hot flame as this Baptist community became a world leader in the foreign missionary enterprise. In the main, their story corroborates the aphorism of C. H. Spurgeon (1834–92) that 'the coals of orthodoxy are necessary to the fire of piety'.[5] What follows is the story of that revival as it impacted the Particular or Calvinistic Baptists.[6]

1

'A very dunghill in society':

The Calvinistic Baptists and their need for revival

There were two main groups of Baptists in the British Isles during the eighteenth century. The one, the General Baptists, were Arminian in theology and had been the first English-speaking Baptists to emerge from the Puritan movement in the early seventeenth century. During the eighteenth century, though, most of this group of Baptist churches became spiritually moribund by their denial of the Trinity. Matthew Caffyn (1628–1714), for instance, was a leading General Baptist pastor who found that his mind was unable to fathom the mystery of the Trinity and that of the deity of Christ, and concluded that neither could be true. By the mid-eighteenth century, Caffyn's way of reasoning was that of the majority of the General Baptists. As Dan Taylor (1728–1816) — a General Baptist who sought, but ultimately failed, to bring renewal to his denomination in the latter part of the eighteenth century — put it: 'they degraded Jesus Christ, and He degraded them.'[1]

The other main group of Baptists was called the Particular Baptists and they were Calvinists. Their first churches had appeared in the late 1630s and early 1640s in London and by 1715 there were some 220 Particular Baptist churches in England and Wales. During the seventeenth century they had been one of the most vigorous evangelistic bodies in the British Isles.[2] But many of them were in decline for much of the eighteenth century.

Calvinistic Baptist pastors who laboured in the middle of the eighteenth century were not reticent to remark on this very evident decline. John Gill (1697–1771), the doyen of Calvinistic Baptists in this period, stated in 1750 in his funeral sermon for his friend Samuel Wilson (1702–50), pastor of Prescot Street Baptist Church, London:

> *The harvest is great, and faithful and painful ministers are few. There are scarcely any that naturally care for the estate and souls of men, and who are heartily concerned for their spiritual welfare... And what adds to the sorrow is, that there are so few rising to fill the places of those that are removed; few that come forth with the same spirit, and are zealously attached to the truths of the everlasting gospel. Blessed be God, there is here and there one that promises usefulness, or otherwise the sorrow and grief at the loss of gospel ministers would be insupportable.[3]*

Gill's younger contemporary, Benjamin Wallin (1711–82), pastor of Maze Pond Particular Baptist Church in London, whose own congregation actually saw an increase in members during his pastorate from 1741 to 1782, frequently made mention of 'the universal complaints of the decay of practical and vital godliness.'[4] Wallin was very conscious of living in a 'melancholy Day', a day of 'present Declensions' amongst Baptist churches.[5]

A somewhat less subjective indicator of decline is the statistics of Calvinistic Baptist congregations for the eighteenth century. For the first couple of decades of the 1700s the major source of statistical evidence is a list of nonconformist congregations drawn up by the Presbyterian minister John Evans between the years

1715 and 1718. While the list is reasonably accurate with regard to paedobaptist congregations, research by W. T. Whitley in the last century turned up a good number of Calvinistic Baptist congregations not listed by Evans.[6] On the basis of the Evans list and his own research, Whitley estimated that there were roughly 220 Calvinistic Baptist congregations in England and Wales around the years 1715 to 1718.[7]

For the determination of Calvinistic Baptist strength at the middle of the century, a survey of fellow Baptist ministers by John C. Ryland (1723–92) in 1753 is especially helpful. Like the Evans list, Ryland's survey is somewhat incomplete. However, an analysis of this survey by Arthur S. Langley has provided some additions to Ryland's figures and indicates that in the early 1750s the number of Calvinistic Baptist congregations had dropped to around 150.[8] From the beginning of the eighteenth century, therefore, there had been a decrease in the number of congregations by approximately one-third. While these figures are only estimates, they do reveal a pattern of decline in the Calvinistic Baptist community during the early decades of the century.[9] Andrew Fuller (1754–1815), who was instrumental in the revitalization of the Baptists in the final decades of the century, summed up this situation in his own inimitable style when he declared that if the situation with the Baptists had continued for much longer, they 'should have been a very dunghill in society'.[10]

Reasons for the decline

Various reasons can be cited for this declension. It would not be surprising that after expending enormous energy in resisting state persecution from 1660 to 1688, even to the point of death in the case of a few pastors and elders, some of the Baptist congregations were simply burnt-out spiritually and mentally unable to engage in aggressive evangelism.[11] Then, it bears remembering that it was illegal for Baptists, or any of the other Nonconformist groups, to engage in mass evangelism outside of their meeting-houses.[12] Thus, their money and effort was poured into the erection of church buildings instead of evangelistic outreach. Moreover, during the time of persecution and thus prior to the erection of a meeting-house, services might be held at a variety of geographical locations and thus a congregation could have an impact over a wide area. But once the building went up, members who lived at a distance were expected to make their way to the meeting-house, and thus the impact in the various locations was somewhat diminished. So it was that the monetary value of the property of the Calvinistic Baptists increased, but its membership was beginning to decrease.[13]

There was also a tendency to get stuck in traditions that had lost their efficacy. Baptists, for instance, were the only major group in eighteenth-century Britain that insisted upon believer's baptism, which, they rightly argued, is the baptism set forth in the New Testament. Anglicans, Congregationalists, Presbyterians and Methodists all upheld infant baptism, while the Quakers dispensed with the rite altogether. Henry Phillips (1719–89), who was brought to faith in Christ under the preaching of fellow Welshman Howel Harris (1714–73) and who later pastored Calvinistic Baptist churches in Ireland and England, well expressed the sentiments of his fellow Baptists when he stated that baptism is 'the door into the church, a sign that one is born again, and brought out of darkness, ignorance and unbelief unto God's marvelous light ... and those who actually profess repentance towards God, faith in Xt. [Christ] & obedience to his commands are the only proper subjects of this ordinance.'[14] When a person was so baptized, therefore, a distinct declaration of belief was being made.

The fact that baptism was traditionally performed outdoors in a pond, stream, or river often made the act an even more forceful

'A very dunghill in society'

declaration. All and sundry could come and watch what was happening and ideally the Baptists would be furnished with an excellent opportunity to bear witness to their distinct convictions. On occasion these public baptisms were performed in weather that was positively inclement. When a young Methodist named Robert Hyde became fully convinced of Calvinism and believer's baptism in December 1782, he made the decision to join the Calvinistic Baptist cause at Colne, Lancashire. The fact that Hyde wanted to be baptized at such a time of year gave one of his friends much concern. After the ice on the water had been broken and just as Hyde was entering the frigid waters, his friend said to him: 'Robert, I think you should wait until the weather is at least a little warmer.' To which Hyde quickly replied, 'I am not certain that I will live to see the warm weather,' and was forthwith baptized. Hyde survived and in time became a valued pastor in nearby Yorkshire.[15]

In some situations, though, an outdoor baptism had a negative effect, but having it outdoors was maintained because of tradition. William Steadman (1764–1837), the great Yorkshire Baptist preacher and educator, records that when he first came into Yorkshire, the older ministers in the county,

> from a foolish scrupulosity ... objected to baptistries in their places of worship, and administered the ordinance in rivers, to whatever disadvantage it might subject them. At Bradford they have baptised in a small stream, the only one near them, scarcely deep enough, muddy at the bottom, and from which the minister and the persons baptised have at least a quarter of a mile to walk along a dirty lane in their wet clothes before they can change. The place likewise, is quite unfavourable for seeing or hearing, and by that means the benefit of the ordinance are lost to the congregation, few of whom ever attend it.[16]

19

There were economic reasons for the decline as well. The strength of the Baptist cause, like other Dissenting communities, lay to a large degree among the working class and when it suffered economically, it is not surprising that this had a residual effect upon Baptist congregations. As one anonymous Dissenter noted in 1731, 'The strength of our interest lies amongst the middling and trading people; and therefore where trade and populousness decrease in a place, our meetings must be expected to grow emptier there.'[17]

Yet another cause of decline was the development of the theological position known as High Calvinism, often called Hyper-Calvinism. Pastors and believers of this persuasion were rightly convinced that salvation is God's work from start to finish. On the basis of this conviction, however, they erroneously reasoned that since unbelievers are unable to turn to Christ, it was unscriptural to urge them to come to the Saviour. Genuinely desirous of exalting God's sovereignty in salvation, Hyper-Calvinist preachers shied away from calling all and sundry to repentance and faith, lest any of the credit for the salvation of sinners go to them. God, in his own time, would convert the elect and bring them into the congregations of the Calvinistic Baptist community.

Andrew Fuller, for instance, whose ministry we will look at in more detail later in this book, was raised in a Baptist work in the small village of Soham, not far from the university town of Cambridge. Its pastor was John Eve (d. 1782), who ministered at Soham from 1752 till his resignation in 1771. Eve was a typical Hyper-Calvinist. His preaching, as Fuller later recalled, 'was not adapted to awaken [the] conscience', and he 'had little or nothing to say to the unconverted'.[18] Thus, despite the fact that Fuller regularly attended the Baptist meeting-house with his family, he gave little heed or thought to the sermons that he heard. Nevertheless, and in spite of his own experience, Fuller found himself preaching much like Eve during the early years of his pastoral ministry. 'Encumbered' with inhibitions, he could not bring himself to offer the gospel indiscriminately to sinners.[19]

A context of revival

Now, it is vital to note that while many Baptists were in this state of declension, from the mid-1730s on there were a series of seemingly separate revivals taking place in Great Britain that ultimately issued in a tremendous stream of revival. The evident spontaneity of these revivals naturally led those participating in them to see them as the result of a rich outpouring of the Holy Spirit.[20] Known as the eighteenth-century Evangelical Revival, or the First Great Awakening in America, the power of this period of revivals is well depicted by two quotes. The first is from the pen of one of the key Welsh leaders in the revival, Howel Harris (1714–73), in a letter that he wrote at the close of 1743 to another central figure in the revivals, the Anglican preacher George Whitefield (1714–70). Writing of the ministry of his fellow Welshmen Daniel Rowland (1711–90) and Howel Davies (*c.* 1716–70) in Wales and under whose preaching Harris had recently sat, the Welshman told Whitefield:

> *The light, divine wisdom, and power to wound and heal, and to reveal the Lord Jesus Christ was such, that words can give no true idea of The outpouring of the Blessed Spirit is now so plentiful and common, that I think it was our deliberate observation that not one sent by Him opens his mouth without some remarkable showers. He comes either as a Spirit of wisdom to enlighten the soul, to teach and build up, and set out the works of light and darkness, or else a Spirit of tenderness and love, sweetly melting the souls like the dew, and watering the graces; or as the Spirit of hot burning zeal, setting their hearts in a flame, so that their eyes sparkle with*

*fire, love, and joy; or also such a Spirit of uncommon power
that the heavens seem to be rent, and hell to tremble.*[21]

The other quote comes from George S. Claghorn, a contemporary
Jonathan Edwards scholar, who has a succinct description of
Whitefield's impact under God on the other side of the Atlantic
in America: 'Wherever he went [from Georgia to Maine], he
drew congregations by the hundreds and thousands. Wholesale
conversions followed, lives were transformed, and a lasting impact
was made on the character of the American people.'[22]

At the heart of these various transatlantic revivals was the Christ-
centred ministry of the Holy Spirit. Fully in line with the New
Testament emphasis about this ministry (see John 16:14a), the
Spirit inspired a profound appreciation for and devotion to the
person and work of the Lord Jesus Christ. As the Spirit of God
moved powerfully throughout British society on both sides of the
Atlantic, tens of thousands of men and women were shaken out of
spiritual slumber and death, and drawn irresistibly to adore and to
serve the Lord Christ.

Baptist response to the revival

Many Calvinistic Baptists, however, had deep reservations about the
revival. The Wesleys, of course, were Arminians and thus beyond
the pale for the *Calvinistic* Baptists. Furthermore, the Wesleys'
view of the Baptists was hardly conducive to good relations. Here is
Charles Wesley in 1756 speaking about the Baptists in his diary. In
his words they were 'a carnal ... contentious sect, always watching
to steal away our children, and make them as dead as themselves'.[23]
However, Whitefield was a Calvinist. Yet, the fervency of his
evangelism and his urging of the lost to embrace Christ, their
only hope of salvation, prompted a number of Baptist critics to
complain of what they termed his 'Arminian accent'.[24]

Most importantly, the Baptists were disturbed by the fact that the earliest leaders in the revival belonged to the Church of England. Their Baptist forebears, after all, had come out of the Church of England at great personal cost and suffering, and they had suffered for their determination to establish true gospel churches. The heritage that came down to the eighteenth-century Calvinistic Baptists was intertwined with a great concern for proper New Testament church order. For example, though writing at the beginning of the century, Benjamin Keach (1640–1704), the second pastor of the congregation that would become the Metropolitan Tabernacle in London, expresses the ecclesiological convictions that prevailed in the Calvinistic Baptist community for much of the eighteenth century. Keach did believe that 'there are many holy and gracious Christians of the communion of the Church of England, and that they are members of the invisible Universal Church',[25] yet he was adamantly opposed to the very concept of a national church established by political fiat.

In his commentary on the parables of Jesus, Keach thus unequivocally stated vis-à-vis Ezekiel 34:14 that this text implies that God's people,

> *shall wander no more on the mountains of error and heresy;*
> *Christ leads them out of all idolatry and superstition, out of*
> *Babylon and all false worship; they shall no more be defiled*
> *with women, that is, by the pollution of false churches, or with*
> *harlot worship; the church of Rome is called the mother of*
> *harlots. Are there no false churches but the Romish church?*
> *Yea, there are, no doubt; she hath whorish daughters, though*
> *not such vile and beastly harlots as the mother is; all churches*
> *that sprang from her, or all of the like nature, in respect of their*
> *constitution, and that retain many of her superstitious names,*
> *garbs, rites, and ceremonies, no doubt they are her daughters.*
> *Were the gospel churches national, or did they receive into*
> *those churches profane persons? No, no, they were a separate*

people, and a congregational and a holy community, being not conformable to this world; and into such a church Jesus Christ brings his sheep. And from hence it followeth, that he carries his lost sheep when he hath found them into his own fold, or into some true gospel church.[26]

Similarly William Herbert (1697–1745), a Welsh Baptist pastor and a friend of Howel Harris, was critical of the latter's decision to stay within the Church of England. In a letter that he wrote to Harris early in 1737, a couple of years after the Evangelical Revival had begun in England and Wales, Herbert likened the Church of England to a pub 'which is open to all comers', and to a 'common field where every noisesome beast may come'. Surely Harris realized, Herbert continued, that the Scriptures — and he has in mind the Song of Solomon 4:12 — describe God's Church as 'a garden enclosed, a spring shut up, a fountain sealed', in other words, a body of believers 'separate from the profane world'?[27] From Herbert's point of view, Harris' commitment to an apostate institution put a serious question mark upon the latter's entire ministry.

Later in the eighteenth century this position was definitively reiterated by the man who was recognized as the leading Calvinistic Baptist divine in the British Isles during the central decades of that era, John Gill. In a pamphlet that Gill had published in 1751 for fellow Baptists in Wales to use specifically in reply to Welsh Anglicans, Gill elaborated on this conviction. The Church of England is not 'a true church of Christ', for she is not congregational in polity, which was 'the form and order of … the first Christian churches', and the doctrine preached in her pulpits is 'very corrupt, and not agreeable to the word of God'.[28] By the latter, Gill was thinking especially of such doctrines as:

eternal election in Christ, particular redemption by him, justification by his imputed righteousness, pardon through

*his blood, atonement and satisfaction by his sacrifice, and
salvation alone by him, and not by the works of men, the
efficacy of divine grace in conversion, the perseverance of the
saints...*[29]

Gill was also disturbed by the practice of infant baptism, certain
aspects in the Anglican celebration of the Lord's Supper, the evident
lack of church discipline, and the use of written prayers.[30] He even
found the Anglican marriage ceremony contrary to the Word of
God, for, he commented, it 'seems to favour the popish notion of
making a sacrament of it, whereas it is a mere civil contract between
a man and a woman, and in which a minister has nothing to do'.[31]
Finally, Gill believed that there could be no communion between
Baptists, and the other Dissenters, and the established Church since
the latter has 'a persecuting spirit', and here the Baptist theologian
recalled the persecution of the Puritans from the time of Elizabeth
I through to the reign of Charles II.[32] The sum of the matter, as far
as Gill was concerned, was that the difference between Anglican
and Baptist is far greater than that between the Roman Catholic
and Anglican.[33] Little wonder, then, that St. Mary's Baptist Church,
Norwich, in 1754 could pass the resolution that 'it is unlawful for
any ... to attend the meetings of the Methodists, or to join in any
worship which is contrary to the doctrines and ordinances of our
Lord Jesus.'[34] Many eighteenth-century Baptists were thus adamant
in their refusal to regard the Evangelical Revival as a genuine work
of God, for, from their perspective, it simply did not issue in 'true
gospel churches'.

Of course, there were some noteworthy exceptions, but up until
the 1770s far too many Calvinistic Baptists seem to have assumed
that a revival could only be considered genuine if it preserved and
promoted the proper form of the local church. For many Calvinistic
Baptists of the first six or seven decades of the eighteenth century,
outward form and inward revival went hand in hand. Their chief

preoccupation was the preservation of what they considered the proper New Testament form of church. In their minds, when God brought revival it would have to issue in true gospel churches like theirs.[35]

The dilemma facing these Baptists was not an easy one. They rightly felt constrained to emphasize the New Testament idea of the local church as a congregation of visible saints and assert that the concept of a state church is antithetical to the whole tenor of the new covenant. Moreover, these were truths for which their forebears in the previous century had suffered much. To abandon them would have been unthinkable. But what then was to be made of the ministry of men like Whitefield?

One possible solution would have been for the eighteenth-century Calvinistic Baptists to have viewed the ministry of Whitefield and other Anglican Calvinists in the way that their seventeenth-century forebears viewed the labours of the sixteenth-century Reformers. The latter did not reject the ministry of the Reformers because they were not Baptists. Rather, they recognized that the Reformers had been greatly used by God to bring the church out of the Stygian darkness of the Middle Ages. Yet, though the Reformers did well, they failed to apply all that the Scriptures taught. As Benjamin Keach said with regard to the Calvinistic Baptist community's recovery of key New Testament principles:

> *Why will not our brethren keep to the great institution, and exact rule of the Primitive church? Must we content our selves with the light which the Church had in respect of this and other Gospel-Truths at the beginning of the Reformation, — since God hath brought forth greater (to the praise of his own rich grace) in our days?*[36]

Similarly, it could have been recognized that God was indeed at work among the leaders of the revival, but that there were certain areas — in particular, those dealing with the church and its nature — where they needed greater light.

Yet, as mentioned above, there were exceptions. In London Andrew Gifford (1700–84) had an extremely fruitful ministry as pastor of Eagle Street Baptist Church from 1735 till his death. A number of years prior to his death some six hundred people had been converted under his preaching and eleven men sent into the pastorate from the congregation. An enthusiastic supporter of both Whitefield and Howel Harris, one hears echoes of their preaching in this extract from the one of the very few sermons of Gifford that has survived. It is a sermon on John 4:14 ('Whosoever drinketh of the water that I shall give him shall never thirst; but the water that I shall give him shall be in him a well of water springing up into everlasting life') and was delivered in 1745. In it Gifford exhorts his hearers:

> If there are any here who have not yet received this living water, let it be improved, by way of advice, earnestly to seek it. Oh, that you did but see your need of it; believe the report, and admit the conviction, that without it you are parched wilderness, barren and dry, nigh unto cursing, whose end is to be burned! ... [But] if ... you are now thro' grace longing to taste of it ... quench not the Spirit, but labour to feel and lay to heart, both the want and worth of it... Above all, go to the spring head the Lord Jesus Christ, whose gift it is... Tell him you come at his invitation and command, and therefore beg he will remember his word, upon which he has encouraged you to hope (Rev. xxii, 17).[37]

Gill on the Trinity

One final point needs making before we leave this subject of Baptist declension. Although John Gill had a hand in this decline, it bears recording that it was this man's theology that was used by God when revival came to the Baptists at the close of the eighteenth century. In a world in which men were abandoning the main contours of biblical orthodoxy — the infallibility of the Word of God, the doctrines of the Trinity, the incarnation and resurrection of Christ — Gill held fast to all of these and enabled the Calvinistic Baptists to weather the intellectual storms of the eighteenth century. And in so doing, his fidelity gave form and shape to the coals of orthodoxy upon which the fire of revival fell later in the century through men like Andrew Fuller.

Take, for example, his robust defence of Trinitarianism. As William C. Placher and Philip Dixon have clearly demonstrated, the growing rationalism of the seventeenth and eighteenth centuries led to a 'fading of the trinitarian imagination' and to the doctrine of the Trinity coming under heavy attack.[38] Informed by the Enlightenment's confidence in the 'omnicompetence' of human reason, the intellectual climate of this era either dismissed the doctrine of the Trinity as a philosophical and unbiblical construct of the post-Apostolic Church, and turned to classical Arianism as an alternate perspective, or simply ridiculed it as utterly illogical, and argued for Deism or Socinianism.[39] Gill's *The Doctrine of the Trinity Stated and Vindicated* — first published in 1731 and then reissued in a second edition in 1752 — proved to be an effective response to this anti-Trinitarianism. In it he sought to demonstrate that there is 'but one God; that there is a plurality in the Godhead; that there are three divine Persons in it; that the Father is God, the Son God, and the Holy Spirit God; that these are distinct in Personality, the same in substance, equal in power and glory'.[40] The heart of this treatise was later incorporated into Gill's *Body of Doctrinal Divinity* (1769), which, for most Baptist pastors of that day, was their major reference work of theology.[41] As John Rippon (1751–1836), Gill's successor at Carter Lane, noted in a biographical sketch of his predecessor:

The Doctor not only watched over his people, *'with great affection, fidelity, and love;' but he also watched his* pulpit *also. He would not, if he knew it, admit any one to preach for him, who was either cold-hearted to the doctrine of the Trinity; or who* denied *the divine filiation of the Son of God; or who* objected *to conclude his prayers with the usual* doxology *to Father, Son, and Holy Spirit, as three equal Persons in the one Jehovah. Sabellians, Arians, and Socinians, he considered as real enemies of the cross of Christ. They* dared *not ask him to preach, nor* could *he in conscience, permit them to officiate for him. He conceived that, by this uniformity of conduct, he adorned the pastoral office.*[42]

He did more than 'adorn the pastoral office'. Through his written works he played a key role in shepherding the English Calvinistic Baptist community along the pathway of biblical orthodoxy.

The Rev. Benjamin Francis A.M.

2

'The Saviour calls':

The ministry and piety of
Benjamin Francis and Anne Steele[1]

The paradigm of spiritual vitality, followed by decline and then revival is one that has been frequently used to explain the course of English Calvinistic Baptist history throughout the late seventeenth and eighteenth centuries. While true for some areas of the English Calvinistic Baptist community, notably London, the Midlands and Yorkshire, it cannot be regarded as the whole story. As we shall see in this chapter, prior to the revival that swept the English Baptist community in the late eighteenth and early nineteenth centuries, those Baptist congregations in the West Country, who comprised what was then called the Western Association, knew something of the spirituality of the revival.[2]

Though this association of churches was not without its ups and downs, its zeal for the gospel, evangelical Calvinism, revival and the visible extension of Christ's kingdom was unflagging.[3] In 1718 and 1719, for example, when a great controversy over subscribing to a Trinitarian creed arose among the Nonconformist churches in Exeter and then later was vociferously debated at Salter's Hall in London, the Western Association asserted the importance of churches subscribing to a confessional statement. Fourteen years later, in 1733, they did this very thing when they renewed their commitment to the *Second London of Confession of Faith* (1677/1689), which had replaced the *First London Confession of Faith* as the doctrinal standard of the Calvinistic Baptists. They subsequently kept up fellowship with one another through the yearly printing of an association letter, a practice later adopted by other Baptist associations.

It was in the geographical heart of this association, at Bristol, that the first Baptist school for training pastors was organized, the Bristol Baptist Academy, initially funded by a generous bequest from the will of Edward Terrill (1635–86), an elder in the Broadmead Church, Bristol. The roll call of alumni from the academy is impressive, a good number of whom had a tremendous impact in the revival of the Calvinistic Baptist cause. As British Baptist historian Raymond Brown has noted:

> *Many of ... [the] Bristol students brought an outstanding contribution to the life of the churches in the second half of the eighteenth century. Men like John Ash (1724–79) of Pershore, Benjamin Beddome (1717–95) of Bourton-on-the-Water and Benjamin Francis of Horsley were content to serve their respective churches for between forty and fifty years, pouring their entire working ministry into the pastoral care of rural congregations, faithful biblical preaching, the development of association life, the establishment of new causes and, in each case, the composition or publication of hymns. Their devotional hymnology, passion for associating, and evangelistic initiatives helped to divert many churches from high Calvinism and introduced them to these influences which were powerfully at work in the Evangelical Revival.*[4]

Let us look more closely at one of these men that Brown mentions, namely, Benjamin Francis (1734–99).[5]

Francis' importance in his day

About a year and a half before John Gill died — whom we met in the previous chapter — he considered the possibility of stepping down from his Southwark pastorate, where he had been since 1719. A number of his congregation were eager for him to have an assistant since he was evidently failing physically. Gill, though, was willing to consider complete retirement if one condition were met, namely, that a Welsh Baptist by the name of Benjamin Francis, pastor of a cause at Horsley, Gloucestershire, could be persuaded to succeed him.[6] Nothing, however, seems to have come of Gill's suggestion during his lifetime. It was only after Gill's death in October of 1771 that Francis was invited to preach at the church. By February 1772, the deacons of the church had made a point of approaching Francis about the possibility of his moving to London. Francis wrote to his fellow Welshman Caleb Evans (1737–91), then tutor at the Bristol Baptist Academy, to express his astonishment at the request.

> *My dear friend, I cannot express the astonishment, the shame, the concern & perplexity, my mind has been overwhelmed with ever since. The thought of parting with my dear people, & of the unhappy consequences that may follow, dissolves my heart, & almost overpowers my spirits; while on the other hand a pleasing prospect of more extensive general usefulness presents itself... I am in a great strait, my mind is in a state of perpetual suspence [sic].*[7]

Francis eventually decided not to go to London. Though he felt 'astonishment' and 'shame' at being asked to succeed Gill, it says much for the respect in which this Welsh pastor was held that he was the first to be considered for the famous London pastorate.

Francis' life and ministry

Unknown to nearly all but a few historians today, Benjamin Francis was in many respects a remarkable individual. He was the youngest son of Enoch Francis (1688–1740), the most respected Welsh Baptist minister of his day and one who 'was extremely gifted in winning hearers'.[8] Orphaned at the age of six, though, the younger Francis was later convinced that he personally experienced God's saving grace when he was but a boy. Baptized at Swansea when he was fifteen, Francis began to preach four years later.

Francis studied in Bristol from 1753 to 1756. When he first arrived in Bristol his knowledge of English was so slight that he could not even return thanks for his food in the language. Bernard Foskett (1685–1758), the principal of the academy, was of the opinion that Francis should be sent back to Wales because of the language barrier. However, the younger tutor at the school, Hugh Evans (1713–81), himself a Welshman who had been converted under the preaching of Enoch Francis, pleaded that Benjamin be allowed to stay. By dint of study Francis eventually obtained a thorough knowledge of English so that he could preach with complete ease in either it or Welsh.

After he graduated, Francis preached for a while in Chipping Sodbury, Gloucestershire. Eventually, in 1757, he moved to Horsley, where the following year he was ordained at the age of twenty-four.[9] Although the church there consisted of 66 members, most of them were poor artisans and clothworkers and were unable to provide enough financially for his support. Francis once described the circumstances of most of the congregation as being 'extremely indigent'. And near the end of his life, he remarked that his congregation was for the most part 'poor, plain, and have not had the advantage of literature'.[10] Thus, 'he was obliged to rear pigs, to grow his own fruit and vegetables, to keep a school, and to venture into the woollen trade (with disastrous financial consequences) in order to make ends meet'.[11]

Alongside these monetary problems, Francis also experienced a long series of domestic trials. In 1765, his first wife and three of their children all died within the space of three months. He married again a year later to an Abigail Wallis. They had ten children, of whom they buried seven![12] In the midst of these deeply distressing circumstances Francis drew comfort from the piety that a number of his dying children exhibited. For instance, when one of the children from his second marriage, Hester, was dying at the age of eleven in August 1790, she told her mother: 'My soul is as full of joy as it can contain — the Lord is become my salvation — the gates of heaven are open to me, and I shall soon be there.' Her last words to her father were: 'I love you, but I love Christ more.'[13]

Despite these deep trials, Francis proved to be a tireless evangelist, one, we are told, who delighted in 'telling poor sinners the unsearchable riches of his compassionate Redeemer'.[14] During his time at Horsley Francis baptized nearly 450 persons who had been converted under his ministry. At the time of his death the number of members in his church was 252. The meeting-house was enlarged three times during Francis' ministry, so that by the early nineteenth century the church was one of the largest in the English Calvinistic Baptist community. Francis attributed much of the success that attended his preaching to the Sunday prayer meetings the church held at six o'clock in the morning and in the afternoon before the afternoon service. Fifty or sixty would come to the Sunday morning prayer meeting, while at the afternoon prayer meeting, the vestry would literally overflow with people.[15]

His indefatigable preaching and evangelism was not limited to Horsley, however. In the biographical sketch of Francis that his son-in-law Thomas Flint (d. 1819) drew up within a few weeks of Francis' death, we are told that:

He was the first means of introducing evangelical religion into many dark towns and villages in all the neighbourhood round [Horsley]. For many years he made excursions monthly into the most uninstructed parts of Gloucestershire, Worcestershire and Wiltshire; besides visiting his brethren, and strengthening their hands in God. In the course of his route through Worcestershire, which he regularly attended from about 1772 to 1784, it appears he had preached in Cheltenham 130 Sermons, at Tewkesbury 136, at Pershore 137, and at Upton upon Severn 180: his manner was to set out from home on Monday morning, and return on Friday evening, after taking a circuit of 90 miles, and preaching every evening. In Wiltshire, on the other side of Horsley, he established a monthly lecture at Malmesbury which he supplied from 1771 to 1799, so that he preached there 282 sermons, and for the latter part of the time he reached as far as Christian-Malford where he had preached 84 sermons. He extended his journey frequently as far as Devizes, 30 miles from home, where he preached 56 times, and oftener to Melksham, Frome, Trowbridge, and Bradford at each of which four places he had preached 90 sermons. At Wotton-under-edge, seven miles from Horsley, he kept up a monthly lecture for thirty years, and preached there 394 times. At Uley, five miles distant, he maintained another stated lecture for many years, and had preached 350 sermons there.[16]

In addition to these extensive labours, he also regularly preached in places as far away as London and Dublin, Portsmouth and Plymouth, as well as undertaking repeated preaching tours of his native Wales. In a day when travel to a town but twenty miles away was a significant undertaking,[17] this record of Francis' itinerant ministry is positively amazing, and parallels the sort of itinerancy that characterizes the Evangelical revivals in the Established Church.

Literary links to the preacher

Regretfully, little remains of Francis' extensive preaching ministry by way of literary texts. We do have some of his poems,[18] including a variety of polemical pieces,[19] and a number of elegies, among them ones for John Gill, George Whitefield, and the 'seraphic' Samuel Pearce (1766–99).[20] There is also a two-volume collection of his hymns in Welsh entitled *Aleluia*. Only a few of them have ever been translated into English.

It is disappointing, however, that none of his sermons appear to have survived. Describing his preaching, Flint emphasizes that Francis was always concerned 'to declare the whole counsel of God', even when he preached for other denominational bodies. Firm in expressing his doctrinal convictions, he was also a compassionate preacher, who often openly wept for his hearers.[21] Possibly the closest we get to hearing his 'melodious voice'[22] is in the circular letters he drew up for the Western Association of Calvinistic Baptist Churches.

Associations of churches in geographical proximity had been a regular feature of Calvinistic Baptist life since the denomination's seventeenth-century beginnings. By the last half of the eighteenth century these associations were holding annual meetings at which representatives of the churches in these associations, usually the pastors and elders, were meeting for a couple of days. These annual meetings would be marked by times of corporate prayer, fellowship, and occasions for the public preaching of the Scriptures. One of Francis' poems, entitled 'The Association', sought to capture the ideals that informed these yearly gatherings.

Thee, bless'd assembly! emblem of the throng
That praise the Lamb in one harmonious song
On Zion's hills where joys celestial flow,
The countless throng redeem'd from sin and woe;
Thee, bless'd assembly, have I oft survey'd,
With sweet complacence, charmingly array'd
In robes of truth, of sanctity and love,
Resembling saints and seraphim above...
 The sacred page thy only rule and guide,
'Thus saith the Lord', shall thy debates decide;
While charity wide spreads her balmy wings
O'er different notions, in indifferent things,
And graceful order, walking hand in hand
With cheerful freedom, leads her willing band...
 In thee, the guardians of the churches' weal,
Whose bosoms glow with unabating zeal,
With balmy counsel their disorders heal,
And truth and love and purity promote
Among the sheep, Immanuel's blood has bought.
 In thee, impartial discipline maintains
Harmonious order, but aloud disclaims
All human force to rule the human mind,
Impose opinions and the conscience bind.[23]

To be sure, this is an idealistic rendition, yet it enables us to see what one eighteenth-century Baptist regarded as important about these annual assemblies. For Francis, they were times when sage advice could be sought and given, when God's people could be free to discuss in love and without rancour non-essential issues on which they disagreed, and when the sole binding force on the conscience was Scripture alone. Most significantly, Francis saw in these gatherings a visible token — in his words, an 'emblem' — of the unity and joy that fills the saints in heaven as they worship Christ the Lamb.

Each of the churches in the association was supposed to send a letter to the annual meeting informing their sister congregations of their state, newsworthy items and prayer concerns. And at some point in the two-day meeting one of the pastors would be chosen to write a letter to all of the churches in the association on behalf of the association itself. It would be ratified, printed after the annual meeting, and sent out as a circular letter. 'A body of divinity in miniature' is the way that the circular letter was described by John Collett Ryland (1723–92) during this period.[24] The Western Association, which had existed since 1653, gave Francis the privilege of writing this letter five times — in 1765, 1772, 1778, 1782 and 1796.[25]

Understandably he touches on a number of themes in these letters — the challenges of poverty and affluence, the dangers of dead orthodoxy, faith and assurance, the need for heart religion, the disciplines of the Christian life, the unity of the local church — but there is one theme that comes up again and again, the beauty of Christ and the passion that should be ours in serving him. In the final analysis, it was this passion for Christ and his glory that underlay all of Francis' evangelistic and pastoral labours.

Christ-centred piety

In the circular letter of 1772 Francis encourages those of his readers 'who are sickly and feeble in the spiritual life' and who are become 'almost strangers to closet devotion, deep contrition for sin, earnest wrestling with the Lord in prayer, heavenly affections, and sensible communion with God' to ask themselves: 'Will you call *this* the religion of Jesus? Is *this* the fruit of his love and crucifixion?'[26] Without a 'living faith in Jesus Christ', Francis reminds them, 'our orthodox notions', church attendance, and outward morality will ultimately avail for nothing. He thus urges upon them their need to have 'a spiritual sight of the awful perfections of God, of the adorable glories of Christ, and of the ineffable excellency of divine and eternal things'.[27]

Moreover, they need to beware of resting their salvation in their performance as Christians and their faithful attendance upon the various ordinances of the Christian life. 'Constantly rest in Christ alone,' Francis says, making use of one of the central watchwords of the Reformation, and so 'look for every blessing … in and thro' him the infinitely prevalent Mediator'.[28] Building on this last point, Francis urges his readers to 'live daily on Christ as your spiritual food, and seek hourly communion with him as the beloved of your souls'.[29] It bears remembering that this counsel was being given to labourers and shopkeepers, croppers and weavers, who spent much of their time simply 'getting by'. Yet, Francis rightly felt that such were capable of living out their daily lives as 'the sincere disciples and intimate friends of Jesus'.[30]

The 1778 circular letter, which is chiefly concerned with the nature of genuine, vital faith, sounds similar notes. In a section of the letter dealing with the differences between assurance and faith, Francis encourages his audience:

> *Place then your entire confidence in Christ for the whole of salvation: Let the declarations and promises of the gospel be your only warrant for believing in him: and consider your purest principles, happiest frames, and holiest duties, not as the foundation, but the superstructure of faith: Let not your sweetest experiences, which are at best but shallow cisterns, but Christ alone be the source of your comfort, and constantly live upon that inexhaustible fountain.*[31]

For the believer, Christ alone is both the source of salvation and the strength for the Christian life. The final clause is, of course, an allusion to Jeremiah 2:13. There, the Lord upbraids his people for forsaking him, 'the fountain of living waters', and living instead on the water drawn from 'broken cisterns' of their own making. Inspired, no doubt, by New Testament passages such as John 4:10–13 and 7:37, where Christ states that he is the source of 'living water' that quenches spiritual thirst, Francis identifies the 'fountain' of Jeremiah 2 as Christ. Christ, not *the believer's* experience of him, is to be the source of the believer's spiritual life.

I close with two further evidences of his Christ-centred piety drawn from letters he wrote in his final years. Writing in October 1796 to a close friend, Daniel Turner (1709–98), pastor of the Calvinistic Baptist work in Abingdon, Oxfordshire, he said:

> *O that my thoughts and affections were more as a well of living water, rising as high as the throne of God and the Lamb! What shall I do with this vain roving heart, which is my daily burden? When shall heaven prevail over earth, and bear away all the pollutions of my corrupt nature? I often think, whatever opinions others may entertain of me, that I am in myself a chaos of ignorance and a mass of deformity. I need the Holy Spirit to enlighten me, and the blood of Christ to cleanse me, and a lively faith in the atoning Lamb, now as much as ever.*[32]

And in a letter to another friend dated 6 November 1798, he declares:

> *O that every sacrifice I offer were consumed with the fire of ardent love to Jesus. Reading, praying, studying and preaching are to me very cold exercises, if not warmed with the love of Christ. This, this is the quintessence of holiness, of happiness, of heaven. While many professors desire to know that Christ loves them, may it ever be my desire to know that I love him, by feeling his love mortifying in me the love of self, animating*

my whole soul to serve him, and, if called by his providence, to suffer even death for his sake.[33]

This Christ-centredness that permeates these writings of Francis is the very atmosphere of the revival that comes to Baptist ranks, as we shall see.

The hymns of Anne Steele

A second example of vital piety is found in the hymns of Anne Steele (1717–78),[34] who was the daughter of William Steele, the pastor of the Calvinistic Baptist chapel in Broughton, Hampshire, a village situated roughly mid-way between Salisbury and Winchester. Converted in 1732 and baptized the same year, she grew to be a woman of deep piety, genuine cheerfulness and blessed with a mind hungry for knowledge. Her piety was wrought in the furnace of affliction. She wrestled most of her adult life, it appears, with ongoing bouts of tertian malaria and terrible stomach pain.[35]

She never married, although there were two proposals of marriage — one from none other than the Baptist pastor and hymnwriter Benjamin Beddome (1717–95). Anne, however, made a conscious choice to remain single. In a letter she wrote to her step-sister after refusing one of these proposals, she said that the suitor had offered his hand to help over the stile, that is, get married. But when she looked over into the meadow of marriage, she writes, 'I looked over and saw no flowers, but observ'd a great many thorns, and I suppose there are more hid under the leaves, but as there is not verdure enough to cover half of 'em it must be near winter, as I think it generally happens when I look into the said Meadow.'[36]

So Anne remained single. But her singleness gave her the time to devote herself to poetry and hymn-writing, a gift with which the Lord had richly blessed her. About ten years before her death, sixty-two of her hymns were published in a Baptist hymnal entitled *A Collection of Hymns Adapted to Public Worship* (1769), whose editors were John Ash and Caleb Evans. This hymnal gave her hymns a wide circulation throughout Baptist circles,[37] and, in time, her hymns became as well known in Baptist circles as those of Isaac Watts (1674–1748), John Newton (1727–1807), or William Cowper (1731–1800).

One of the very few of her hymns that is still sung today reveals the way in which this wide circulation of her hymns would have played a part in revitalizing areas of the Calvinistic Baptist cause throughout England. It was originally entitled 'The Saviour's Invitation', and was based on Jesus' words in John 7:37: 'If any man thirst, let him come unto me, and drink' (KJV).

> The Saviour calls — let every Ear
> Attend the heavenly Sound;
> Ye doubting Souls, dismiss your Fear,
> Hope smiles reviving round.
>
> For every thirsty, longing Heart,
> Here Streams of Bounty flow,
> And Life, and Health, and Bliss impart,
> To banish mortal Woe.
>
> Here, Springs of sacred Pleasure rise
> To ease your every Pain,
> (Immortal Fountain! full Supplies!)
> Nor shall you thirst in vain.
>
> Ye Sinners come, 'tis Mercy's Voice,
> The gracious Call obey;
> Mercy invites to heavenly Joys, —
> And can you yet delay?

Dear Saviour, draw reluctant Hearts,
To Thee let Sinners fly;
And take the Bliss Thy Love imparts,
And drink, and never die.[38]

Based on Jesus' open invitation to sinners to come to him and drink, that is, find eternal life, Steele urges 'every Ear' to 'attend' to Christ's heavenly invitation. He calls all who are 'thirsty' and 'longing' to come to him, where they will find 'Life, and Health, and Bliss,' in sum, 'Springs of sacred Pleasure' that will ease every woe. This invitation is a command — 'the gracious Call obey' — and a free offer — 'can you yet delay?'[39] But Steele is also aware that the 'thirsty, longing Heart' is not sufficient in itself to come to Christ. In the final analysis it is a 'reluctant Heart', filled with doubt and fear. Hence, she prays, 'Dear Saviour, draw reluctant hearts'. And this is a prayer that can be prayed with confidence,

Anne Steele's grave in St Mary's Church, Broughton, Hampshire

for the Saviour to whom she speaks is an 'Immortal Fountain', Mercy incarnate who loves sinners and delights in bestowing on them 'heavenly joys'. As Baptist men and women of England sang such hymns, God was preparing them for the 'reviving' that we are about to consider in the next chapters.

John Ryland Jr (1753–1825)

3

'A little band of brothers':

Friendship and revival in the life of John Ryland Jr

Revival and reformation are rarely, if ever, wrought by God through one individual, contrary to the impression given by some popular church histories. Collegiality is central to times of spiritual blessing. As James Davison Hunter argues in his book, *To Change the World: The Irony, Tragedy, and Possibility of Christianity in the Late Modern World*, the 'great man of history' view, namely, that 'the history of the world is but the biography of great men' is wrong.[1] Rather, 'the key actor in history is not individual genius but rather the network [of individuals and friends] and the new institutions that are created out of those networks.' Hunter thus maintains that 'charisma and genius and their cultural consequences do not exist outside of networks of similarly oriented people and similarly aligned institutions.'[2]

A superb illustration in church history of the truth of Hunter's thesis is the revival of the English Baptist community in the late eighteenth century that we are thinking about in this book. Christopher Anderson (1782–1852), a Scottish Baptist leader who became a close friend of a number of those who were centrally involved in these momentous events, reckoned,

...that in order to much good being done, co-operation, the result of undissembled love, is absolutely necessary; and I think that if God in his tender mercy would take me as one of but a very few whose hearts he will unite as the heart of one man — since all the watchmen cannot see eye to eye — might I be but one of a little band of brothers who should do so, and who should leave behind them a proof of how much may be accomplished in consequence of the union of only a few upon earth in spreading Christianity, oh how should I rejoice and be glad! In order to such a union, however, I am satisfied that the cardinal virtues, and a share of what may be considered as substantial excellence of character, are absolutely necessary, and hence the importance of the religion which we possess being of that stamp which will promote these. Such a union in modern times existed in [Andrew] Fuller, [John] Sutcliff, [Samuel] Pearce, [William] Carey, and [John] Ryland. They were men of self-denying habits, dead to the world, to fame, and to popular applause, of deep and extensive views of divine truth, and they had such an extended idea of what the Kingdom of Christ ought to have been in the nineteenth century, that they, as it were, vowed and prayed, and gave themselves no rest.[3]

For much of the eighteenth century, as noted above, far too many Baptist churches in England, Wales and Ireland were moribund and without vision for the future or passion for the salvation of the lost at home or abroad. Definite tendencies towards 'Hyper-Calvinism', an introspective piety that was a reaction to the Enlightenment of that era, and an inability to discern God's hand at work in the Calvinistic Methodist revivals of their day, as well as various social and political factors were central in their decline. By the first decade of the next century, however, the low-burning embers in their churches had been fanned into white-hot flame as this Baptist community became a world leader in the foreign missionary enterprise, an enterprise that became identified with one name in particular, namely that of William Carey (1761–1834). The man whose writings, above all others, provided the theological underpinnings for this revival was Andrew Fuller, who, because of the weightiness of his theological influence and acumen, has been rightly called 'the elephant of Kettering'.[4] But, and this is vital to recognize, neither he nor Carey accomplished what they did by themselves alone.

There is little doubt in the mind of this author that Fuller's friendship with a number of like-minded Baptist pastors from the Midlands — in particular the elder Robert Hall (1728–91) of Arnesby, John Sutcliff (1752–1814), of Olney, John Ryland Jr of Northampton, Samuel Pearce of Birmingham, and William Carey — was indispensable to the transformative impact of his theology. These men took the time to think and reflect together, as well as to encourage one another and pray together. 'An aversion to the same errors, a predilection for the same authors, with a concern for the cause of Christ at home and abroad'[5] bound these men together in a friendship that was a significant catalyst for both renewal and revival. If we had time we could examine the network of relationships between these men, this 'little band of brothers' as Anderson puts it, and see Hunter's thesis clearly fleshed out. Due to space constraints, though, the focus of this chapter will be on the friendship of two members of this band of brothers, John Ryland and Andrew Fuller.

Friendship in contemporary western culture and that of the ancient world

Our culture is not one that provides great encouragement for the nurture and development of deep, long-lasting, satisfying friendships. Such friendships take time and sacrifice, and western culture in the early twenty-first century is a busy world that as a rule is far more interested in receiving and possessing than sacrificing and giving.[6] Roger Scruton, the conservative public commentator and philosopher who specializes in aesthetics, has rightly noted in a recent interview that westerners 'are living through … a decline in real friendship'.[7] Now, what is especially disturbing about this fact is that western Christianity is little different from its culture. The English Anglican writer C. S. Lewis (1898–1963) has an ingenious little book entitled *The Screwtape Letters*, a remarkable commentary on spiritual warfare from the point of view of our Enemy. In it there is one letter from the senior devil, Screwtape, to his nephew Wormwood in which Screwtape rejoices over the fact that 'in modern Christian writings' there is to be found 'few of the old warnings about Worldly Vanities, the Choice of Friends, and the Value of Time'.[8] Now, whether or not Lewis is right with regard to a scarcity of twentieth-century, Christian literature about 'Worldly Vanities' and 'the Value of Time', he is undoubtedly correct when it comes to the topic of friendship.

How different in this respect is our world from that of the ancients, both pagan and Christian. In the ancient world, friendship was deemed to be of such vital importance that the pagan philosopher Plato devoted an entire book, the *Lysis*, as well as substantial portions of two other books, the *Phaedrus* and the *Symposium*, to a treatment of its nature. Aristotle, the other leading thinker of the classical Greek period, also considered the topic of friendship significant enough to have a discussion of it occupy two of the ten books of the *Nicomachean Ethics*, his major work on ethical issues. For the ancient Greeks — and this is true also of the Romans — friendship formed one of the highest ideals of human life.

Though we do not find such extended discussions of the concept of friendship in the Scriptures, we do come across reflections on friendship like Ecclesiastes 4:7-12 as well as marvellous illustrations of what a true friendship looks like. For instance, there is the friendship of Ruth and Naomi that cuts across generations, or that of David and Jonathan, or in the New Testament, Paul and Timothy. There are also nuggets of advice about having friends and keeping them in that Old Testament compendium of wisdom, Proverbs. One comes away from texts like these with the impression that the world of the Bible regards friendship as a very important part of life.

Two central images are found in the biblical representation of friendship.[9] The first is that friendship involves *the knitting together of souls*. Deuteronomy provides the earliest mention of this when it describes 'a friend who is as your own soul' (Deuteronomy 13:6), that is, a friend is a companion of one's innermost thoughts and feelings. This is well illustrated by Jonathan and David's friendship, described for us in 1 Samuel 18:1-4. Here, in this text, we see that the privileges and responsibilities of a biblical friend entail strong emotional attachment and loyalty.

The second metaphor that the Bible uses to represent friendship is *the face-to-face encounter*. This is the image used, for example, of Moses' relationship to God. In the tabernacle God spoke to Moses 'face to face, as a man speaks to his friend' (Exodus 33:11; see also Numbers 12:8). The image of a face-to-face encounter implies conversation, a sharing of confidences and consequently a melding together of minds, goals and direction. One of the benefits of such face-to-face encounters between friends is the heightened insight that such encounters produce. As Proverbs 27:17 famously puts it: 'Iron sharpens iron, and one friend sharpens another.'

An excellent example of a friendship that has both of these scriptural characteristics is that between John Ryland Jr and Andrew Fuller.

The younger Ryland

Ryland's father was the Baptist minister, John Collett Ryland (1723–92), who had a voracious appetite for learning. For much of his life the elder Ryland was pastor of College Lane Baptist Church, Northampton, and one of the leading Calvinistic Baptist lights of the eighteenth century.[10] He seems to have sought to stimulate a similar appetite for books and learning in his children, in particular, in his namesake, John Ryland Jr. And it worked, for the son recalled that as a young child, he 'was fond of reading, and generally preferred that employment to play'. The elder Ryland's piety also influenced his son. Though at times quite eccentric, the father was an ardent lover of the Lord Jesus. 'What a glory to be connected with all the infinite good in Christ,' he wrote on one occasion in a small piece enumerating encouragements to pray.[11] Thus, learning and devotion were interwoven early on in the life of the younger Ryland.[12]

The younger Ryland was converted and baptized in 1767.[13] He spoke for the first time before his father's church in May of 1770 — he was but seventeen years old. Many years later he would say that he had 'had very few silent Sabbaths since'.[14] Ryland was invited by College Lane in 1781 to become co-pastor with his father. When his father moved five years later to Enfield, near London, Ryland became the sole pastor.[15] Ryland himself moved from Northampton in 1793. He went to Bristol where, until his death in 1825, he was the pastor of Broadmead Church and the principal of Bristol Baptist Academy, both positions being held concurrently.[16] The year before he moved to Bristol, Ryland had played a key role in the founding of what would come to be called the Baptist Missionary Society that sent Carey and his family to India. His closest friend Andrew Fuller was the first secretary of this society, and when Fuller died in 1815, Ryland succeeded him.

An outstanding Hebrew scholar and solid preacher, Ryland exercised a significant influence on the lives of the two hundred or so students who studied at Bristol during his time as principal. The student body was never huge at any one time. In 1816 for example, there were 22 students studying at the school.[17] Yet, the majority of them went on to become Baptist pastors and missionaries, imbued with Ryland's evangelical Calvinism and commitment to revival. Over time Ryland became one of the respected pillars of Calvinistic Baptist life in England. On one occasion, when Robert Hall Jr (1764–1831), his successor, was told something he regarded as incredible, Hall asked on whose authority was the report based. When he was told it was on that of Ryland, he replied, 'Did Ryland say so, Sir? Then it is true, Sir; for I would as soon receive his testimony as the affidavit of seven archangels.'[18]

Since we shall look at Fuller's life and ministry in more detail in chapter 5, here we must suffice with noting that Fuller's infrangible commitment to live under the authority of the infallible Scriptures, along with his lifelong study of the works of the American divine Jonathan Edwards (1703–58), eventuated in his becoming 'the soundest and most creatively useful theologian the Particular Baptists have ever had'.[19]

A Baptist friendship

Ryland and Fuller first met in 1778 when both of them were young men and they were wrestling with a number of extremely important theological issues. Within a year they were the closest of friends. After Fuller moved to Kettering in 1782 the two of them had frequent opportunities to talk, to pray and to spend time together, for Northampton and Kettering are only thirteen miles apart. Their friendship was to be unbroken for the next thirty-seven years, till Fuller's death in 1815.

In the year that he died, Fuller described his relationship with Ryland as a 'long and intimate friendship' that he had 'lived in, and hoped to die in'.[20] And nine days before he died, Fuller asked one last request of Ryland: would he preach his funeral sermon? Ryland agreed, though it was no easy task for him to hold back his tears as he spoke.[21] Towards the end of this sermon, Ryland reminisced about the fact that their friendship had 'never met with one minute's interruption, by one unkind word or thought, of which I have any knowledge' and that the wound caused by the loss of 'this most faithful and judicious friend' was something that would never be healed in this life.[22] Ryland's statement that his friendship with Fuller had 'never met with one minute's interruption, by one unkind word or thought' is quite an amazing statement and speaks volumes about the way these two men treasured their relationship.

The cost of their friendship

The year following Fuller's death, Ryland published a biography of his close friend. In the introduction, Ryland stated the following about their friendship: 'Most of our common acquaintance are well aware, that I was his oldest and most intimate friend; and though my removal to Bristol, above twenty years ago, placed us at a distance from each other, yet a constant correspondence was all along maintained; and, to me at least, it seemed a tedious interval, if more than a fortnight elapsed without my receiving a letter from him'.[23] When Ryland moved to Bristol in 1793 he was no longer close enough to his friend in Kettering for them to meet on a regular basis. The only way that they could keep their friendship alive and intact was through the medium of the letter. Thus, for more than twenty years, they faithfully corresponded with one another, and Ryland notes, if he did not hear from Fuller at least once every two weeks he found it 'tedious', that is, painful and upsetting.[24] Both Ryland and Fuller evidently knew that their friendship was a fragile treasure that could be so easily lost or neglected in the rush of life if they did not give it the attention it needed. As the American preacher Haddon Robinson has noted: 'Even strong friendships require watering or they shrivel up and blow away.'[25]

Friendship — warts and all

What had initially attracted Ryland and Fuller to one another was the discovery that they shared 'a strong attachment to the same religious principles, a decided aversion to the same errors, a predilection for the same authors,'[26] in particular, Jonathan Edwards. In other words, they had that fundamental aspect of a good friendship: a union of hearts. They found deep joy in their oneness of soul — their passion for the glory of Christ and the extension of his kingdom. But friends are not Siamese twins or clones of one another. It belongs to the essence of genuine friendship that friends accept one another for what they are, warts and all, and they give one another room to disagree.[27]

In the case of Ryland and Fuller their main difference of opinion revolved around what was an extremely volatile issue among the transatlantic English-speaking Baptists of the eighteenth-century world: the twin issues of open and closed communion and open and closed membership.[28] In the eighteenth century the vast majority of pastors and congregations in the Calvinistic Baptist denomination, including Fuller, adhered to a policy of closed membership — that is, only baptized believers could become members of their local churches — and closed communion — that is, only baptized believers could partake of the Lord's Supper in their meeting-houses.[29] Ryland, on the other hand, was of the conviction that both the Lord's Supper and membership in the local church should be open to all Christians, regardless of whether or not they had been baptized as believers. He was thus committed to a policy of both open communion and open membership. When Ryland was the pastor of the College Lane Church in Northampton, for instance, one of the leading deacons of the church, a certain Thomas Trinder, did not receive believer's baptism until six years after he had been appointed deacon.[30] Fuller would never have tolerated such a situation in the church at Kettering. But Ryland and Fuller were secure enough in their friendship to disagree and not have it destroy their friendship.

Quarrel over Serampore

The only time that this theological difference really came close to disturbing their friendship was in connection with the Baptist Missionary Society's mission at Serampore, India.[31] Headed by William Carey, Joshua Marshman (1768–1837), and William Ward (1769–1823) — all of whom were friends of Ryland and Fuller — this mission adopted a policy of open communion in 1805. Writing to Fuller that year, the Serampore missionaries informed him they had come to the conviction that 'no one has a right to debar a true Christian from the Lord's table, nor refuse to communicate with a real Christian in commemorating the death of their common Lord, without being guilty of a breach of the Law of Love'. 'We cannot doubt', they went on to affirm, 'whether a Watts, an Edwards, a Brainerd, a Doddridge, a Whitefield, did right in partaking of the Lord's Supper, though really unbaptized, or whether they had the presence of God at the Lord's Table?'

Fuller was deeply disturbed by this reasoning and the decision made by the Serampore missionaries, and exerted all of his powers of influence and reasoning to convince them to embrace closed communion, which they eventually did in 1811. Ryland, though, was not slow to criticize this reversal of policy. But, as he later said of his disagreement with Fuller: 'I repeatedly expressed myself more freely and strongly to him, than I did to any man in England;

yet without giving him offence.'[32] It is also noteworthy that Carey did not take offence at Fuller either. When he heard of Fuller's death in 1815, he wrote almost immediately to Ryland and told him: 'I loved him very sincerely. There was scarcely another man on the Earth to whom I could so compleatly [sic] lay open my heart as I could to him.'[33]

We are all subject to the temptation to make our views about secondary matters far more important than they actually are and to squeeze our friends into our own mould when it comes to these issues. Fuller and Ryland, on the other hand, genuinely knew how to give each other space to disagree on what many of their Baptist acquaintances regarded as an all-essential issue.

The one essential Friendship

When Fuller lay dying in April 1815, he was asked if he wanted to see Ryland, his oldest living friend in England. His response was terse: 'He can do me no good.'[34] His reply seems to be an odd statement, lacking in appreciation for what their friendship had meant to the two men. But it needs to be understood in context. In his final letter to Ryland, Fuller had begun by saying: 'We have enjoyed much together, which I hope will prove an earnest of greater enjoyment in another world ... [There] I trust we shall meet, and part no more.'[35] Clearly, his feelings about his friendship with Ryland had undergone no alteration whatsoever. In the light of his impending death, however, there was only one friendship which he knew to be needful in that moment: his friendship with the Triune God — Father, Son and Holy Spirit. As another eighteenth-century writer, an Anglican rector by the name of James Newton, had written when faced with the death of his brother: 'If we have God for our Friend, what need we to fear, Nothing, but without his Friendship we may be looked on as the most miserable of Men.'[36]

The silhouette of John Sutcliff (1752–1814)

4

'I wish I had prayed more':

John Sutcliff and the Concert of Prayer for revival

How does renewal or revival come to a Christian community or congregation? A variety of answers can be given to this important question, but, from the vantage-point of church history, prayer will head the list. When God's people are driven to realize their desperate need for spiritual advance and revival, they also realize they must pray for this to happen. Only God can do the work of God, and true revival is his work. As such, they cry out to God, both corporately and singly, for God to stretch forth his arm and revive his people. A great example of this important truth can be found in the English Baptist community of the eighteenth century that is the subject of this book.

Now, among the Calvinistic Baptist figures of this period one of the most important is also one of the least known — John Sutcliff, the pastor of the Baptist church in Olney, Buckinghamshire, for thirty-nine years. An extremely close friend of both Andrew Fuller and William Carey, as we have noted in the previous chapter, and one of the founders of the Baptist Missionary Society, Sutcliff played a central part in bringing revival to the English Calvinistic Baptists through the medium of prayer.

Early years in West Yorkshire

Sutcliff's early nurture in the Christian faith came through his parents, Daniel and Hannah Sutcliff, both of whom attended Rodhill End Baptist Church, not far from Hebden Bridge, Yorkshire.[1] But it was not until 1767 or 1768, when Sutcliff was either sixteen or seventeen, that he was converted during a local revival in Wainsgate Baptist Church, where his parents worshipped on alternate weeks, since there was a service at Rodhill End only every other week. The pastor of the church, John Fawcett (1740–1817), had himself been converted through the preaching of George Whitefield (1714–70), and was shaped as a young Christian by the eccentric Anglican evangelical William Grimshaw (1708–63).[2] According to his son, Fawcett kept a portrait of Whitefield in his study and 'the very mention of his name inspired the warmest emotions of grateful remembrance.'[3] Fawcett was thus personally convinced of many of the emphases of the Evangelical Revival, and would in time become a powerful force for revival in the north of England.

After a couple of years under Fawcett's watchful care, Sutcliff devoted two and half years, from 1772 to May of 1774, to theological study at Bristol Baptist College. He then briefly served in two Baptist churches, one in Shrewsbury and one in Birmingham, before he entered upon what would be his life's ministry at Olney, Buckinghamshire, in July 1775.

Reading Jonathan Edwards

John Sutcliff began to study in earnest the writings of Jonathan Edwards (1703–58), rightly known as the theologian of revival and described by Miklós Vetö as 'the greatest Christian theologian of the eighteenth century',[4] not long after he came to Olney. First introduced to the writings of Edwards by John Fawcett, the works of this New England divine exercised a great influence in shaping Sutcliff's theology. Edwards' writings first gave Calvinists like Sutcliff an answer to the Enlightenment critique that divine sovereignty and human freedom are incompatible. Human beings, Edwards argued, refused to obey God not because of any natural inability. Rather, it was their affections that were enslaved and needed to be re-oriented in godly directions. Then, Edwards also maintained that the duty incumbent upon all who heard the gospel was immediate repentance. As a Calvinist, Edwards upheld the utter necessity of grace in conversion. But he moved away from the passive understanding of conversion that had prevailed in some seventeenth-century Calvinist quarters, and that was still very much a part of Hyper-Calvinism in the eighteenth century, and argued sinners must respond to the gospel summons without delay. The upshot of Edwardsean Calvinism was a dual commitment to revival at home and strenuous missionary endeavours abroad.[5]

It was this evangelical Calvinism of Jonathan Edwards that led Sutcliff to the conviction that certain aspects of the Hyper-Calvinism that was then regnant in many Calvinistic Baptist churches were unscriptural. For instance, a number of Sutcliff's fellow pastors denied that it was the *duty* of sinners to believe in the Lord Jesus. They reasoned that since the Scriptures ascribe repentance and faith to the working of the Holy Spirit, neither of these can be regarded as duties required of sinners. In practical terms, this meant that the preaching of these pastors omitted 'the free invitations of the gospel' and thus 'chilled many churches to their very soul'.[6] Edwards' writings particularly helped Sutcliff to be convinced of 'the harmony … between the duty of ministers to call on sinners to repent and believe in Christ for salvation, and the necessity of omnipotent grace to render the call effectual'.[7]

Sutcliff soon began to incorporate into his preaching these fresh insights regarding the relationship between human responsibility and divine grace. Some of his congregation, however, were deeply disturbed by what they considered to be a departure from the canons of 'orthodoxy', and they began to absent themselves from the church's celebration of the Lord's Supper. But Sutcliff was not to be deterred from preaching biblical truth, and 'by patience, calmness, and prudent perseverance' he eventually won over all those in this congregation who stood opposed to his theological position.

As we have noted in the previous chapter, Sutcliff's commitment to Edwardsean Calvinism was shared by a number of other pastors in the geographical vicinity of Olney. In particular this included John Ryland Jr at College Street Baptist Church in Northampton, whom Sutcliff had met in the early 1770s, and Andrew Fuller at Kettering Baptist Church, whom Sutcliff first met in 1776 at the annual meeting of the Northamptonshire Association, to which the churches of all three pastors belonged.

In the spring of 1784, Ryland shared with Sutcliff and Fuller a treatise of Edwards which had been sent to him by the Scottish Presbyterian minister John Erskine (1721–1803).[8] When Erskine was in his mid-twenties he had entered into correspondence with Edwards, and long after Edwards' death in 1758 he had continued to uphold Edwards' theological perspectives and to heartily recommend his books. Well described as 'the paradigm of Scottish evangelical missionary interest through the last half of the eighteenth century',[9] Erskine regularly corresponded with Ryland from 1780 until his death in 1803, sending him not only letters, but also, on occasion, bundles of interesting books and tracts which he sought to promote. Thus it was in April 1784 that Erskine mailed to Ryland a copy of Edwards' *An Humble Attempt to Promote Explicit Agreement and visible Union of God's People in Extraordinary Prayer for the Revival of Religion and the Advancement of Christ's Kingdom on Earth, Pursuant to Scripture-Promises and Prophecies*

Concerning the Last Time (henceforth referred to as the *Humble Attempt*). The *Humble Attempt* was not widely heeded during the lifetime of its author. Its greatest impact would come after Edwards' death. As Iain H. Murray has noted, it is arguable that no such tract on the hidden source of all true evangelistic success, namely, prayer for the Spirit of God, has ever been so widely used as this one.[10]

The Prayer Call of 1784

Reading Edwards's *Humble Attempt* in the spring of 1784 had a profound impact on Ryland, Fuller and Sutcliff. Fuller was to preach that June at the annual meeting of the Northamptonshire Association. On his way to the meeting at Nottingham, Fuller found that heavy rains had flooded a number of spots of the roads over which he had to travel. At one particular point the flooded area appeared so deep that Fuller was reluctant to continue. A resident of the area, who knew how deep the water actually was, encouraged him to urge his horse through the water. 'Go on sir,' he said, 'you are quite safe.' As the water came up to Fuller's saddle, Fuller began to have second thoughts about continuing. 'Go on, sir,' the man said again, 'all is right.' Taking the man at his word, Fuller continued and safely traversed the flooded area of the road. This experience prompted Fuller to abandon the sermon he had planned to preach. Instead he spoke on 2 Corinthians 5:7 at the association meeting: 'We walk by faith, not by sight.'[11]

During the course of this sermon, which Fuller entitled, 'The Nature and Importance of Walking by Faith', Fuller clearly revealed the impression Edwards' *Humble Attempt* had made upon his thinking when he appealed thus to his hearers:

Let us take encouragement, in the present day of small things, by looking forward, and hoping for better days. Let this be attended with earnest and united prayer to Him by whom Jacob must arise. A life of faith will ever be a life of prayer. O brethren, let us pray much for an outpouring of God's spirit upon our ministers and churches, and not upon those only of our own connection and denomination, but upon 'all that in every place call upon the name of Jesus Christ our Lord, both theirs and ours' (1 Cor. 1:2).[12]

At the same meeting, Sutcliff proposed that the churches of the association establish monthly prayer meetings for the outpouring of God's Holy Spirit and the consequent revival of the churches of Great Britain. This proposal was adopted by the representatives of the sixteen churches at the meeting, and on the last page of the circular letter sent out that year to the churches of the association there was what has come to be known as 'The Prayer Call of 1784', which was most likely drawn up by Sutcliff.[13] The entire document runs as follows:

Upon a motion being made to the ministers and messengers of the associate Baptist churches assembled at Nottingham, respecting meetings for prayer, to bewail the low estate of religion, and earnestly implore a revival of our churches, and of the general cause of our Redeemer, and for that end to wrestle with God for the effusion of his Holy Spirit, which alone can produce the blessed effect, it was unanimously RESOLVED, to recommend to all our churches and congregations, the spending of one hour in this important exercise, on the first Monday in every calendar month.

We hereby solemnly exhort all the churches in our connection, to engage heartily and perseveringly in the prosecution of this plan. And as it may be well to endeavour to keep the same hour, as a token of our unity herein, it is supposed the following scheme may suit many congregations, viz. to meet on the first Monday evening in May, June, and July, from 8 to 9. In Aug. from 7 to 8. Sept. and Oct. from 6 to 7. Nov. Dec. Jan. and Feb. from 5 to 6. March, from 6 to 7; and April, from 7 to 8. Nevertheless if this hour, or even the particular evening, should not suit in particular places, we wish our brethren to fix on one more convenient to themselves.

We hope also, that as many of our brethren who live at a distance from our places of worship may not be able to attend there, that as many as are conveniently situated in a village or neighbourhood, will unite in small societies at the same time. And if any single individual should be so situated as not to be able to attend to this duty in society with others, let him retire at the appointed hour, to unite the breath of prayer in private with those who are thus engaged in a more public manner.

The grand object of prayer is to be that the Holy Spirit may be poured down on our ministers and churches, that sinners may be converted, the saints edified, the interest of religion revived, and the name of God glorified. At the same time, remember, we trust you will not confine your requests to your own societies [i.e. churches]; or to your own immediate connection [i.e. denomination]; let the whole interest of the Redeemer be affectionately remembered, and the spread of the gospel to the most distant parts of the habitable globe be the object of your most fervent requests. We shall rejoice if any other Christian societies of our own or other denominations will unite with us, and do now invite them most cordially to join heart and hand in the attempt.

Who can tell what the consequences of such an united effort in prayer may be! Let us plead with God the many gracious promises of His Word, which relate to the future success of His gospel. He has said, 'I will yet for this be enquired of by the

*House of Israel to do it for them, I will increase them with
men like a flock.' Ezek. xxxvi.37. Surely we have love enough
for Zion to set apart one hour at a time, twelve times in a year,
to seek her welfare.*[14]

There are at least four noteworthy points about this Prayer Call.
First, very much in evidence in this statement, as well as in the
extract from Fuller's sermon, is the conviction that any reversal of
the decline of the Calvinistic Baptists could not be accomplished
by mere human zeal, but must be effected by the Spirit of God.
As Sutcliff noted in another context in strongly Edwardsean
language:

*The outpouring of the divine Spirit ... is the grand promise of
the New Testament ... His influences are the soul, the great
animating soul of all religion. These withheld, divine ordinances
are empty cisterns, and spiritual graces are withering flowers.
These suspended, the greatest human abilities labour in vain,
and noblest efforts fall success.*[15]

Then there is the catholicity that is recommended with regard
to the subjects of prayer. As the Calvinistic Baptists of the
Northamptonshire Association gathered together to pray, they
were encouraged not to think simply of their own churches and
their own denomination, but they were to embrace in prayer
believers of other denominational bodies. The kingdom of God
consists of more than Calvinistic Baptists! In fact, churches of
other associations were encouraged to join with them in praying
for revival. This was a quite a break from earlier Baptist attitudes
towards those of the established Church, for example. Only thirty-
five years earlier Gill had argued for a position that refused to
countenance open communion with Anglicans. And here this
prayer call is urging prayer with them for revival. If, as is likely,
Sutcliff wrote this document, the catholicity recommended is

understandable from his own context in Olney, where he and the Anglican minister, who was none other than John Newton of later fame, were often in each other's company and even traded pulpits at the new year.

Third, there is the distinct missionary emphasis of the Prayer Call. The members of the association churches were urged to pray that the gospel be spread 'to the most distant parts of the habitable globe'. Little did these Baptists realize how God would begin to fulfil these very prayers within the space of less than a decade.

Finally, the sole foundation for praying for revival is located in the Scriptures. Only one text, Ezekiel 36:37, is actually cited though, but those issuing this call to prayer are aware of 'many gracious promises' in God's Word which speak of the successful advance of his kingdom. At first glance this passage from Ezekiel hardly seems the best text to support the Prayer Call. But the overall context of this verse needs to be considered. It is one in which God is telling Israel that he will bring them back from exile in Babylon to the promised land. Before he does this, however, he tells his people that he will stir them up to pray for this very return from exile. Sutcliff and his fellow Baptists have rightly discerned the principle that preceding times of revival and striking extensions of Christ's kingdom there invariably occur the concerted and constant prayers of Christians.

The return of prayers

The association meetings at which this Prayer Call was issued were held on 2–3 June 1784. At the end of that month, on 29 June, the church that Sutcliff pastored in Olney resolved to establish a 'monthly meeting for prayer ... to seek for a revival of religion'.[16] Two years later, Sutcliff gave the following progress report and exhortation regarding the prayer meetings that had been established in his own church and others in the association.

> *The monthly meetings of prayer, for the general spread of the gospel, appear to be kept up with some degree of spirit. This, we hope, will yet be the case. Brethren, be not weary in well-doing, for in due time ye shall reap, if ye faint not. We learn that many other churches, in different, and some in distant parts of the land, and some of different denominations, have voluntarily acceded to the plan. We communicate the above information for your encouragement. Once more we would invite all who love truth and holiness, into whose hands our letter may fall, to unite their help. Let societies, let families, let individuals, who are friends to the cause of Christ unite with us, not only daily, but in a particular manner, at the appointed season. With pleasure we were informed of an open door in many places, for the preaching of the gospel. We request it of our friends that they would encourage the occasional ministry of the word in their respective villages and neighbourhoods, where they may be situated, to the utmost of their power. Be not backward to appear on God's side.*[17]

As this text shows, Sutcliff, like his mentor Edwards, was convinced that not simply the individual prayers of God's people presaged revival, but the prayers of God's people when they gathered together to pray in unison.[18] And, as Sutcliff went on to indicate, God was already answering their prayers by providing 'an open door in many places, for the preaching of the gospel'.[19]

The passing years did not diminish Sutcliff's zeal in praying for revival and stirring up such prayer. For instance, Ryland wrote in his diary for 21 January 1788:

> *Brethren Fuller, Sutcliff, Carey, and I kept this day as a private fast, in my study … and each prayed twice*[20] — *Carey with*

singular enlargement and pungency. Our chief design was to implore a revival of godliness in our own souls, in our churches, and in the church at large.[21]

And in 1789, the number of prayer meetings for revival having grown considerably, Sutcliff decided to bring out an edition of Edwards' *Humble Attempt* to further encourage those meeting for prayer. Measuring only six and one quarter inches long, and three and three-quarter inches wide, and containing 168 pages, this edition was clearly designed to be a handy pocket-size edition. In his 'Preface' to this edition, Sutcliff reemphasized that the Prayer Call issued by the Northamptonshire Association five years earlier was not intended for simply Calvinistic Baptists. Rather, they ardently wished it might become general among the real friends of truth and holiness.

The advocates of error are indefatigable in their endeavours to overthrow the distinguishing and interesting doctrines of Christianity; those doctrines which are the grounds of our hope, and sources of our joy. Surely it becomes the followers of Christ, to use every effort, in order to strengthen the things, which remain ... In the present imperfect state, we may reasonably expect a diversity of sentiments upon religious matters. Each ought to think for himself; and every one has a right, on proper occasions, to shew [sic] his opinion. Yet all should remember, that there are but two parties in the world, each engaged in opposite causes; the cause of God and Satan; of holiness and sin; of heaven and hell. The advancement of the one, and the downfall of the other, must appear exceedingly desirable to every real friend of God and man. If such in some respects entertain different sentiments, and practice distinguishing modes of worship, surely they may unite in the above business. O for thousands upon thousands, divided into small bands in their respective cities, towns, villages, and neighbourhood, all met at the same time, and in pursuit of one end, offering up

> *their united prayers, like so many ascending clouds of incense before the Most High! — May he shower down blessings on all the scattered tribes of Zion! Grace, great grace be with all them that love the Lord Jesus Christ in sincerity!* [22]

In this text Sutcliff positions the Prayer Call of 1784 on the broad canvas of history, in which God and Satan are waging war for the souls of men and women. Prayer, because it is a weapon common to all who are 'friends of truth and holiness', is one sphere in which Christians can present a fully united front against Satan. Sutcliff is well aware that evangelicals in his day held differing theological positions and worshipped in different ways. He himself was a convinced Baptist — convinced, for instance, that the Scriptures fully supported congregational polity and believer's baptism — yet, as he rightly emphasizes in the above 'Preface', such convictions should not prevent believers, committed to the foundational truths of Christianity, uniting together to pray for revival.

Hard on the heels of the republication of Edwards' treatise came the events leading to the formation of the Particular Baptist Society for the Propagation of the Gospel among the Heathen in 1792, later known as the Baptist Missionary Society. Included among the items recommended for prayer in the Prayer Call of 1784 had been 'the spread of the gospel to the most distant parts of the habitable globe'. God began to answer that specific prayer in the early 1790s. First, God provided a man with the desire to go and evangelize peoples to whom the name of Christ was completely unknown, namely, William Carey. And then, the Lord gave other believers the strength and courage to support him as he went and laboured.[23] Over the next four decades Carey's example would spur numerous others to offer themselves for missionary service. Of these missionary candidates, a good number would be sent to Sutcliff to be tutored by him in a parsonage seminary that he opened at the close of the 1790s.

In 1794, two years after the formation of the Baptist Missionary Society, John Rippon (1750–1836), pastor of Carter Lane Baptist Church in Southwark, London, published a list of Calvinistic Baptist congregations and ministers in his *Baptist Annual Register*. Rippon estimated that there were at that time 326 churches in England and 56 in Wales, more than double the number which had existed in 1750.[24] He printed another list of churches four years later, according to which the numbers had grown to 361 churches in England and 84 in Wales.[25] Reflecting on these numbers, Rippon wrote, 'It is said, that more of our meeting houses have been enlarged, within the last five years, and built within the last fifteen, than had been built and enlarged for thirty years before.'[26]

Rippon was not exaggerating. There was indeed steady growth among the Calvinistic Baptists during the last four decades of the eighteenth century, but it was not until the final decade of the century that there was a truly rapid influx of converts.[27] It is surely no coincidence that preceding and accompanying this growth were the concerts of prayer that many churches had established in response to the Prayer Call of 1784.

'I wish I had prayed more'

On the fiftieth anniversary of the founding of the Baptist Missionary Society, F. A. Cox (1783–1853), reflecting on the origins of the society, stated that:

> The primary cause of the missionary excitement in Carey's mind, and its diffusion among the Northamptonshire ministers [was] … the meeting of the Association in 1784, at Nottingham, [when] it was resolved to set apart an hour on the first Monday evening of every month, 'for extraordinary prayer for revival of religion, and for the extending of Christ's

kingdom in the world'. This suggestion proceeded from the venerable Sutcliff. Its simplicity and appropriateness have since recommended it to universal adoption; and copious showers of blessing from on high have been poured forth upon the churches.[28]

From the vantage point of the early 1840s, Cox saw the Prayer Call of 1784 as pivotal in that it focused the prayers of Calvinistic Baptist churches in the Northamptonshire Association on the nations of the world, and thus prepared the way for the emergence of the Baptist Missionary Society and the sending of Carey to India. Yet he also notes that the 'universal adoption' of the concert of prayer by churches beyond the ranks of the Calvinistic Baptist denomination had led to rich times of revival, when God poured forth upon these churches 'copious showers of blessing'. Later historians would describe this period of blessing as the Second Evangelical Awakening (1790s–1830s). Some of them, like J. Edwin Orr and Paul E. G. Cook, would concur with Cox and rightly trace the human origins of this time of revival and spiritual awakening to the adoption of the concert of prayer by the Calvinistic Baptists in 1784.[29]

However, in one area Cox's statement in somewhat misleading. In describing Sutcliff as 'the venerable Sutcliff' he leaves the reader with an idyllic impression of the Baptist pastor. How sobering to find that this man, who was at the heart of a prayer movement that God used to bring so much spiritual blessing to his church, also struggled when it came to prayer. When Sutcliff lay dying in 1814 he said to Fuller: 'I wish I had prayed more.'[30] For some time Fuller ruminated on this statement by his dying friend. Eventually he came to the conviction that Sutcliff did not mean that he 'wished he had prayed more frequently, more *spiritually*.' Then Fuller elaborated on this interpretation by applying Sutcliff's statement to his own life:

'I wish I had prayed more'

*I wish I had prayed more for the influence of the Holy Spirit;
I might have enjoyed more of the power of vital godliness. I
wish I had prayed more for the assistance of the Holy Spirit, in
studying and preaching my sermons; I might have seen more
of the blessing of God attending my ministry. I wish I had
prayed more for the outpouring of the Holy Spirit to attend the
labours of our friends in India; I might have witnessed more
of the effects of their efforts in the conversion of the heathen.*[31]

Whether or not Fuller correctly interpreted Sutcliff's statement, his
application certainly resonates with themes dear to Sutcliff's heart:
personal renewal, the revival of the church, and Spirit-empowered
prayer and witness.

Andrew Fuller (1754–1815)

5

'A dull flint':

Andrew Fuller and theological reformation

The Holy Spirit, who is the Spirit of life and the giver of new life, is also the Spirit of truth. And he never comes with his breathing of new life and renewal into Christian communities like the one we are considering without also bringing his truth. So times of renewal and revival are also times when biblical truth comes to the fore: old truths are rediscovered, and false, though not necessarily heretical, ideas are replaced with the robust truths of Holy Scripture.

When revival came to the Baptists at the close of the eighteenth century, it involved, among other things, a trenchant critique of Hyper-Calvinism, which was one of the factors stymieing growth of the Baptists. The key figure that God used in this regard was Andrew Fuller,[1] whose theology ultimately prepared the way for William Carey to go to India. In a 1991 article in *Christianity Today* Bruce Shelley looked at five unsung heroes who stood behind five famous leaders in church history. And he rightly included Fuller as 'the unsung hero' behind Carey's 'pioneering missionary career in Asia'.[2] Though long forgotten in many Baptist circles, it bears remembering that Fuller was once described by Charles Haddon Spurgeon (1834–92) as 'the greatest theologian' of his century.[3]

And Southern Baptist historian A. H. Newman on one occasion commented that Fuller's 'influence on American Baptists' was 'incalculable' for good.

Fuller wrote major theological works on a variety of issues, many of them in the area of apologetics. Indeed, he excelled when he took up the gauntlet thrown down by the various theological errors of the eighteenth century, aberrations such as Hyper-Calvinism, Socinianism, Deism and Sandemanianism.[4] As he once remarked about himself: 'I am a dull flint, you must strike me against a steel to produce fire.'[5] Philip Roberts, the former president of Midwestern Baptist Theological Seminary in Kansas City, Missouri, has rightly noted in a study of Fuller as a theologian:

> *[Fuller] helped to link the earlier Baptists, whose chief concern was the establishment of ideal New Testament congregations, with those in the nineteenth century driven to make the gospel known worldwide. His contribution helped to guarantee that many of the leading Baptists of the 1800s would typify fervent evangelism and world missions … Without his courage and doctrinal integrity in the face of what he considered to be theological aberrations, the Baptist mission movement might have been stillborn.*[6]

'I will trust … my sinful, lost soul in his hands'

The youngest of three brothers, Andrew Fuller was born on 6 February 1754, at Wicken, a small village now on the edge of the Cambridgeshire Fens, about six miles from the cathedral city of Ely. His parents, Robert Fuller (1723–81) and Philippa Gunton (1726–1816), rented and worked a succession of dairy farms.[7] Baptists by conviction, both of them came from a Dissenting background, of which there were various congregations in the area.

When Fuller was seven years of age, his family moved to the village of Soham, about two and a half miles from Wicken. Once settled in Soham, they joined themselves to the Calvinistic Baptist work in the village that met for worship in a rented barn.[8] The pastor of the work was a certain John Eve (d. 1782), originally a sieve-maker from Chesterton, near the town of Cambridge. Eve had been set apart to preach the gospel by St. Andrew's Street Baptist Church, Cambridge, in 1749,[9] and three years later he was ordained as the first pastor of the Baptist cause at Soham, where he ministered for nearly twenty years till his resignation in 1771.

Fuller later remarked that Eve was a Hyper-Calvinist or, as he put it, one whose teaching was 'tinged with false Calvinism'.[10] As such, Eve did not believe that it was the duty of the unregenerate to exercise faith in Christ. To be sure, they could be urged to attend to outward duties, such as hearing God's Word preached or being encouraged to read the Scriptures, but nothing of a spiritual nature could be required of them, since they were dead in sin and only the Spirit could make them alive to spiritual things.[11] Eve's sermons, Fuller thus noted, were 'not adapted to awaken [the] conscience' and 'had little or nothing to say to the unconverted'.[12]

When he was fourteen, though, Fuller began to entertain thoughts about the meaning and purpose of life. He was much affected by passages that he read from the biography of John Bunyan (1628–88), his *Grace Abounding to the Chief of Sinners*, as well as Bunyan's *Pilgrim's Progress* and some of the works of Ralph Erskine (1685–1752), the Scottish evangelical and Presbyterian minister. These affections were often accompanied by weeping and tears, but they ultimately proved to be transient, there being no radical change of heart.

Now, one popular expression of eighteenth-century Calvinistic Baptist spirituality was the notion that if a scriptural text forcefully impressed itself upon one's mind, it was to be regarded as a promise from God. One particular day in 1767 Fuller had such an experience. Romans 6:14 ('sin shall not have dominion over you; for ye are not under the law, but under grace') came with such suddenness and force that Fuller naïvely believed that God was telling him that he was in a state of salvation and no longer under the tyranny of sin. But that evening, he later recalled, 'I returned to my former vices with as eager a gust as ever.'[13]

For the next six months, he utterly neglected prayer and was as wedded to his sins as he had been before this experience. When, in the course of 1768, he once again seriously reflected upon his lifestyle, he was conscious that he was still held fast in thralldom to sin. What then of his experience with Romans 6:14? Fuller refused to doubt that it was given to him as an indication of his standing with God. He was, he therefore concluded, a converted person, but backslidden. He still lived, though, with never a victory over sin and its temptations, and with a total neglect of prayer. 'The great deep of my heart's depravity had not yet been broken up,' he later commented about these experiences of his mid-teens.[14]

In the autumn of 1769 Fuller once again came under the conviction that his life was displeasing to God. He could no longer pretend that he was only backslidden. 'The fire and brimstone of the bottomless pit seemed to burn within my bosom,' he later declared. 'I saw that God would be perfectly just in sending me to hell, and that to hell I must go, unless I were saved of mere grace.' Fuller now recognized the way that he had sorely abused God's mercy. He had presumed that he was a converted individual, but all the time he had had no love for God and no desire for his presence, no hunger to be like Christ and no love for his people. On the other hand, he could not bear, he said, 'the thought of plunging myself into endless ruin'. It was at this point that Job's resolution — 'though he slay me, yet will I trust in him' (Job 13:15) — came to mind, and Fuller grew determined to cast himself upon the mercy of the Lord Jesus 'to be both pardoned and purified'.[15]

Yet, the Hyper-Calvinism that formed the air that he had breathed since his earliest years proved to be a real barrier to his coming to Christ. It maintained, as we have seen, that in order to flee to Christ for salvation, the 'warrant' that a person needed to believe that he or she would be accepted by Christ was a subjective one. Conviction of one's sinfulness and deep mental anguish as a result of that conviction were popularly regarded by Hyper-Calvinists as such a warrant. From this point of view, these experiences were signs that God was in the process of converting the individual that was going through them. The net effect of this teaching was to place the essence of conversion and faith not in believing the gospel, 'but in a persuasion of our being interested in its benefits'. Instead of attention being directed away from oneself towards Christ, the convicted sinner was turned inwards upon himself or herself to search for evidence that he or she was being converted.[16] Against this perspective Fuller would later argue that the gospel exhortation to believe in Christ was a sufficient enough warrant to come to the Lord Jesus.

Fuller was in the throes of a genuine conversion and quite aware of his status as a sinner, but, under the influence of the Hyper-Calvinist spirituality of conversion, he was convinced he had neither the qualifications nor the proper warrant to flee to Christ in order to escape the righteous judgement of God. Upon later reflection, he saw his situation as akin to that of Queen Esther. She went into the presence of her husband, the Persian King Ahasuerus, at the risk of her life, since it was contrary to Persian law to enter the monarch's presence uninvited. Similarly, Fuller decided: 'I will trust my soul, my sinful, lost soul in his [i.e. Christ's] hands — if I perish, I perish!' So it was in November 1769 that Fuller found peace with God and rest for his troubled soul in the cross of Christ.[17]

His personal experience prior to and during his conversion ultimately taught him three things in particular. First, there was the error of maintaining that only those sinners aware of and distressed about their state have a warrant or right to come to Christ. Second, genuine faith is Christ-centred, not a curving inwards upon oneself to see if there was any desire to know Christ and embrace his salvation. Third, he recognized that true conversion is rooted in a radical change of the affections of the heart and manifest in a lifestyle that seeks to honour God.[18]

'To feel my way out of a labyrinth'[19]

The following spring, 1770, Fuller was baptized and joined the church at Soham. Within six years the church had called Fuller to be their pastor. Now, though he had personally known the deadening effect of Hyper-Calvinistic preaching, Fuller knew no other way of

Soham Baptist Church, Soham, Cambridgeshire

dealing with non-Christians from the pulpit and initially, he said, he 'durst not … address an invitation to the unconverted to come to Jesus'.[20] But as he studied the style of preaching exhibited in the Acts of the Apostles and especially in Christ's ministry, he began to see that 'the Scriptures abounded with exhortations and invitations to sinners'. But how was this style of preaching to be reconciled with the biblical emphasis on salvation being a sovereign work of grace?[21]

By 1780 Fuller had come to see clearly that his own way of preaching was unduly hampered by a concern not to urge spiritual duties upon non-believers. As he wrote in his diary for 30 August of that year:

> *Surely Peter and Paul never felt such scruples in their addresses as we do. They addressed their hearers as men — fallen men; as we should warn and admonish persons who were blind and on the brink of some dreadful precipice. Their work seemed plain before them. Oh that mine might be so before me!*[22]

The 'pulpit', Fuller commented a few months later:

> *seems an awful place! — An opportunity for addressing a company of immortals on their eternal interests — Oh how important! We preach for eternity. We in a sense are set for the rising and falling of many in Israel … Oh would the Lord the Spirit lead me into the nature and importance of the work of the ministry!* [23]

And by the time that Fuller left Soham to take up the pastorate of the Baptist work in Kettering, Northamptonshire, he was convinced, as he told the Kettering congregation at his induction on 7 October 1783, that, *it is the duty of every minister of Christ plainly and faithfully to preach the gospel to all who will hear it. And, as I believe the inability of men to spiritual things to be wholly of the moral, and therefore of the criminal kind — and that it is their duty to love the Lord Jesus Christ and trust in him for salvation, though they do not — I, therefore, believe free and solemn addresses, invitations, calls, and warnings to them, to be not only consistent, but directly adapted, as means in the hands of the Spirit of God to bring them to Christ. I consider it as a part of my duty, which I could not omit without being guilty of the blood of souls.*[24]

This theological revolution in Fuller's sentiments about the duty of sinners to believe the gospel and how that gospel should be preached were later encapsulated in a book, *The Gospel of Christ Worthy of All Acceptation* (1785), and in his lifetime his views came to be known as Fullerism. As Geoffrey F. Nuttall once observed, Fuller is thus one of the few Englishmen to have a theological perspective named after him and it 'points to a remarkable achievement'.[25]

'Cordial belief of what God says … [is] every one's duty'[26]

Two editions of *The Gospel of Christ Worthy of All Acceptation* were issued in Fuller's lifetime. A first draft had been written by 1778, the manuscript of which has been purchased by The Southern Baptist Theological Seminary. Just before Christmas 2010 a friend alerted me to an item that was for sale by a rare book dealer, The Philadelphia Rare Books & Manuscripts Co. It was entitled 'Thoughts on the Power of Men to do the Will of God' and was listed as being by Andrew Fuller. As it turns out, they had acquired a manuscript that had been housed since 1860 in the divinity school in Rochester, when it was given to that school by the son of Andrew Fuller, and were asking nine hundred dollars for it.

They could have asked, I think, nine thousand dollars for it. It is invaluable. It is now in the Archives at SBTS, where a digital copy of it will be made. It begins thus:

> *What a narrow Path is Truth! How many Extremes are there into which we are liable to run! Some deny Truth; others hold it, but in Unrighteousness. O Lord, impress thy Truth upon my Heart with thine own Seal, then shall I receive it as in itself it is, 'A Doctrine according to Godliness'.*

This draft was eventually re-written and published as the first edition in Northampton in early 1785. It bore a lengthy subtitle — 'The Obligations of Men Fully to Credit, and Cordially to Approve, Whatever God Makes Known, Wherein is Considered the Nature of Faith in Christ, and the Duty of Those where the Gospel Comes in that Matter'. A second edition appeared in 1801 with a shortened title — *The Gospel Worthy of All Acceptation* — and simpler subtitle, 'The Duty of Sinners to Believe in Jesus Christ', which well expressed the overall theme of both editions of the book.[27] There were a number of substantial differences between the two editions, which Fuller freely admitted and which primarily related to the doctrine of particular redemption, but the major theme remained unaltered: 'faith in Christ is the duty of all men who hear, or have opportunity to hear, the gospel'.[28] Or as he put it in his preface to the first edition:

> *true faith is nothing more nor less than an hearty or cordial belief of what God says, surely it must be every one's duty where the gospel is published, to do that. Surely no man ought to question or treat with indifference any thing which Jehovah hath said.*[29]

What is quickly evident in both of the editions is the large amount of space given to closely reasoned exegesis.

In the first edition, for example, Fuller devotes the second major part of the work to showing that 'faith in Christ is commanded in the Scriptures to unconverted sinners'.[30] It had been reflection on Psalm 2, for instance, that had first led Fuller to doubt the Hyper-Calvinist refusal to countenance faith as the duty of the unconverted.[31] He now undertook an interpretation of this text in light of his subject, reading it, as the New Testament reads it in Acts 4, as a Messianic psalm. The command to 'the heathen' and 'the people' of Israel (v. 1) as well as to 'the kings of the earth' and 'the rulers' (v. 2) — interpreted in Acts 4:27 as 'Herod, and Pontius Pilate, with the gentiles, and the people of Israel' — to 'kiss the Son' (v. 12) is a command given to those 'who were most certainly enemies to Christ, unregenerate sinners'. And 'kissing the Son' Fuller understood to be 'a spiritual act', which meant, from the perspective of the New Testament, nothing less than 'being reconciled to, and embracing the Son of God, which doubtless is of the very essence of true saving faith'.[32] Clearly, Fuller reasoned, here was both Old and New Testament support for his position.

A number of Johannine texts, however, plainly revealed that 'true saving faith' is 'enjoined [by the New Testament] upon unregenerate sinners'.[33] John 12:36, for instance, contains an exhortation of the Lord Jesus to a crowd of men and women to 'believe in the light' that they might be the children of light. Working from the context, Fuller argued that Jesus was urging his hearers to put their faith in him. He is the 'light' in whom faith is to be placed, that faith which issues in salvation (John 12:46). Those whom Christ commanded to exercise such faith, however, were rank unbelievers, of whom it is said earlier 'they believed not on him' (John 12:37), and, in fact, Fuller pointed out on the basis of the quote of Isaiah 6:10 in John 12:40, 'it seems' that these very same people whom Christ called to faith in him 'were given over to judicial blindness, and were finally lost'.[34]

Then there is John 6:29, where Jesus declares to sinners that 'this is the work of God, that ye believe on him whom he hath sent'. Fuller pointed out that this statement is made to men who in the context are described as following Christ simply because he gave them food to eat (v. 26) and who are considered by Christ to be unbelievers (v. 36). Christ rebukes them for their mercenary motives and urges them to 'labour not for the meat which perisheth, but for that meat which endureth unto everlasting life' (v. 27). Their response as recorded in John 6:28 is to ask Christ: 'What shall we do, that we might work the works of God?' His answer is to urge them to put their faith in him (v. 29). It is as if, Fuller said, Christ had told them, faith in him is 'the first duty incumbent' upon them 'without which it will be impossible … to please God'.[35]

Again, in John 5:23 Fuller read that all men and women are to 'honour the Son, even as they honour the Father'. Giving honour to the Son entails, Fuller reasoned, 'holy hearty love to him' and adoration of every aspect of his person. It necessarily 'includes faith in him'. Christ has made himself known as a supreme monarch, an advocate who pleads the cause of his people, a physician who offers health to the spiritually sick, and an infallible teacher. Therefore, honouring him in these various aspects of his ministry requires faith and trust.[36]

Among the practical conclusions that followed from such scriptural argumentation was that preachers of the gospel must passionately exhort their hearers to repent and commit themselves to Christ.[37] In the second edition, Fuller sharpened this emphasis, for he was more than ever convinced that there was 'scarcely a minister amongst us' — that is, amongst the Calvinistic Baptist denomination — 'whose preaching has not been more or less influenced by the lethargic systems of the age'.[38] Far too many of Fuller's fellow Baptist ministers failed to imitate the preaching of Christ and the apostles who used to exhort the unconverted to immediate repentance and faith. For a variety of reasons, they regarded the unconverted in their congregations as 'poor, impotent … creatures'. Faith was beyond such men and women, and could not be pressed upon them as an immediate, present duty. Fuller was convinced that this way of conducting a pulpit ministry was unbiblical and simply helped the unconverted to remain in their sin.[39] Without a doubt Fuller's conclusion that ministers needed to press home repentance and faith as immediate duties upon all of their hearers was foundational to Carey's later argument that this needed to take place not only in England but throughout the world.[40] Chadwick Mauldin is surely right when he affirms that *The Gospel Worthy of All Acceptation* was 'at its heart a missionary document'.[41]

Village preaching

It needs noting that Fuller's convictions in *The Gospel Worthy of All Acceptation* were not merely theoretical.[42] His journal after beginning his ministry at Kettering reveals that he was putting into practice what he argued in that epoch-making book. Not only was he urging sinners at Kettering to put their faith in Christ, but from April 1784 to December 1784, for instance, Fuller noted in his diary that he had preached in no less than thirty-three different villages near and around Kettering.[43] The following journal entries illustrate the prominence that village preaching had assumed in his ministry:

> *Nov. 21, 1785. — For above a fortnight past, I have been chiefly out in journies [sic] to Bedford, Arnsby, Bosworth, Eltington, Guilsborough, and Spratton. Preached at each of these places with more or less earnestness. Came home, on Friday, and spoke, with some tenderness, from 'Hold thou me up, and I shall be safe.' On Lord's day, I preached on* the evil nature and dangerous tendency of mental departures from God, *from Prov. xiv. 14. Also, on soul-prosperity, from 3 John 2. Had a tender and earnest mind.*[44]

[January] 15 [,1786]. — Preached, at home, on keeping the Sabbath, *from Isa. lviii. 13, 14. At night, went to Warkton, and with more than usual feeling and affection, preached from Luke xiii. 3. On Tuesday preached at Geddington, about* blind Bartimeus [sic]: *next morning, rode to Bedford, and to Shefford with Brother Sutcliff, where I preached, on* putting on the Lord Jesus. *Felt some pleasure there, in company with some other ministers, in advising the people to moderation in their opposition to a minister who is now a probationer at S — . Heard Mr. Carver at Southhill, and preached at Bedford. Returned home on Friday. I have heard since of the sermon at Bedford, on* soul-prosperity, *being blessed to the conversion of a poor man.*[45]

'The armies of the Lamb'[46]

There is also a direct line from the publication of the *Gospel of Christ Worthy of All Acceptation* to Fuller's wholehearted involvement in the formation of what became the Baptist Missionary Society in October of 1792, which sent Carey to India in 1793, and Fuller's subsequent service as secretary of that society until his death in 1815. The work of the mission consumed an enormous amount of Fuller's time as he regularly toured the country, representing the mission and raising funds. On average he was away from home three months of the year. Between 1798 and 1813, for instance, he made five lengthy trips to Scotland for the mission as well as undertaking journeys to Wales and Ireland.[47] Consider one of these trips, that he made to Scotland in 1805. In less than sixty days, Fuller travelled thirteen hundred miles and preached fifty sermons for the cause of the Baptist mission. He also carried on an extensive correspondence both to the missionaries on the field and to supporters at home. Finally, he supervised the selection of missionary appointees and sought to deal with troubles as they emerged on the field. In short, he acted as the pastor of the missionaries sent out.[48] The amount of energy and time this took deeply worried his friends. As Robert Hall Jr put it in a letter to John Ryland Jr:

> *...if he [i.e. Fuller] is not more careful he will be in danger of wearing himself out before his time. His journeys, his studies, his correspondcies [sic] must be too much for the constitution of any man.*[49]

As he poured himself into the work of the Baptist Missionary Society, Fuller continued to refine his thinking about missions. Along with his re-thinking of the responsibility of both preachers and hearers of the gospel discussed above, there emerged a fresh perspective on the nature of the church. There is little doubt that Fuller wholly affirmed traditional Calvinistic Baptist thinking about the church. In that tradition the church is a body of people who have personally repented and exercised faith in Christ, and borne witness to this inner transformation by baptism.[50] But Fuller was also concerned to emphasize something else about the church.

When Fuller spoke of the local church after he had assumed the role of secretary of the mission his emphasis often fell on the church's responsibility to evangelize and indeed participate in taking the gospel to the ends of the earth. As he wrote, for example, in 1806:

> *The primitive churches were not mere assemblies of men who agreed to meet together once or twice a week, and to subscribe for the support of an accomplished man who should on those occasions deliver lectures on religion. They were men gathered out of the world by the preaching of the cross, and formed into society for the promotion of Christ's kingdom in their own souls and in the world around them. It was not the concern of the ministers or elders only; the body of the people were interested in all that was done, and, according to their several abilities*

and stations, took part in it. Neither were they assemblies of heady, high-minded, contentious people, meeting together to argue on points of doctrine or discipline, and converting the worship of God into scenes of strife. They spoke the truth; but it was in love: they observed discipline; but, like an army of chosen men, it was that they might attack the kingdom of Satan to greater advantage. Happy were it for our churches if we could come to a closer imitation of this model![51]

Fuller certainly had no wish to abandon either the stress on doctrinal preaching for the edification of God's people or that on proper discipline, but he had rightly noted that the pursuit of these concerns to the exclusion of evangelism had produced in all too many eighteenth-century Calvinistic Baptist churches contention, bitter strife and endless disputes. These inward-looking concerns had to be balanced with an outward focus on the extension of Christ's kingdom.

Moreover, evangelism was not simply to be regarded as the work of only 'the ministers or elders'. The entire body of God's people were to be involved. This conception of the church is well summed up in another text, which, like the one cited above, compares the church of Christ to an army. 'The true churches of Jesus Christ,' he wrote five years before his death, 'travail in birth for the salvation of men. They are the armies of the Lamb, the grand object of whose existence is to extend the Redeemer's kingdom.'[52] Retaining the basic structure of earlier Baptist thinking about the church, Fuller has added one critical ingredient drawn from his reading about the life of the Church in the New Testament: the vital need for local Baptist churches to be centres of vigorous evangelism.

'I loved him'

Among the things that William Carey said when he heard of the death of Andrew Fuller were three simple words: 'I loved him.'

Why do I love him and commend his writings to you? Not because he was perfect as a Christian, nor because I always agree with him in every theological jot and tittle. But I love him for three reasons.

First of all, he had that quality that is so necessary for solid pastoral ministry: theological balance. He was at once a zealous missionary theologian, as we have seen, and an ardent upholder of the doctrines of grace. As he wrote to John Ryland Jr, shortly before his death: 'I have preached and written much against the abuse of the doctrine of grace, but that doctrine is all my salvation and all my desire. I have no other hope than from salvation by mere sovereign, efficacious grace through the atonement of my Lord and Saviour.'

Second, Fuller had the ability to nurture and sustain deep, long-lasting, and satisfying friendships that enabled him and his friends to serve God powerfully in their generation. No great work for God is accomplished by men working in isolation. And together these men saw revival. By 1798 there were close to 445 Calvinistic Baptist churches in England and Wales. This number had risen to well over by 1811, and in 1851 it stood at over 1,300.[53]

From a more personal angle, one can observe the revival that was taking place in the following extracts from the letters of Andrew Fuller.[54] In the year 1810 Fuller noted in a letter to William Carey: 'I preached a sermon to the youth last Lord's Day from 1 Thess 2:19. I think we must have had nearly one thousand. They came from all quarters. My heart's desire and prayer for them is that they may be saved.' Fuller was still rejoicing when he wrote to John Ryland on 28 December: 'I hope the Lord is at work among our young people. Our Monday and Friday night meetings are much thronged.' A couple of months later he told Ryland: 'The Friday evening discourses are now, and have been for nearly a year, much thronged, because they have been mostly addressed to persons under some concern about their salvation.' And what was happening in Fuller's church was happening in Baptist causes throughout the length and breadth of England and Wales.

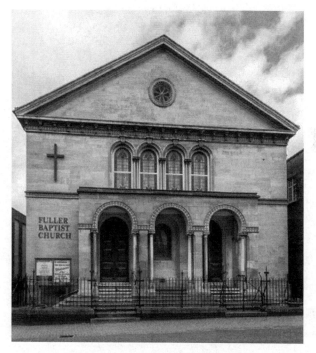

Fuller Baptist Church, Kettering

Finally, Fuller models for us what true Christian piety is all about: he built his life and thought on the Word of God — as he said in the first draft of *The Gospel Worthy of All Acceptation*: 'O Lord, impress thy Truth upon my Heart with thine own Seal.' And he exemplified the great goal of Christian living, which is to live for the glory of the Triune God. As he once said: to 'glorify God, and recommend by our example the religion of the meek and lowly Jesus, are the chief ends for which it is worthwhile to live.'[55]

Samuel Pearce (1766–99)

6

'What a soul!'

The revival piety of Samuel Pearce

Times of revival often produce men and women of pronounced piety. One thinks of the mid-eighteenth-century revivals and David Brainerd (1718–47), for instance, or those of Scotland in the mid-nineteenth century and Robert Murray M'Cheyne (1813–43). The revival that we are considering in this book also bore fruit in a man of remarkable piety, Samuel Pearce. This man's life and thought represent the best of late eighteenth-century Baptist piety. His memoirs, drawn up in 1800 by Andrew Fuller, one of his closest friends, went through innumerable printings and editions on both sides of the Atlantic in the course of the nineteenth century. Another friend, William Jay (1769–1853), who exercised an influential ministry in Bath for the first half of the nineteenth century, said of Pearce's preaching: 'When I have endeavoured to form an image of our Lord as a preacher, Pearce has oftener presented himself to my mind than any other I have been acquainted with'. He had, Jay went on, a 'mildness and tenderness' in his style of preaching, and a 'peculiar unction'. When Jay wrote these words it was many years after Pearce's death, but still, he said, he could see his appearance in his mind's eye and feel the impression that he made upon his hearers as he preached. Ever one to appreciate the importance of having spiritual individuals as one's friends, Jay has this comment about the last time that he saw Pearce alive: 'What a savour does communion with such a man leave upon the spirit.'[1]

David Bogue and James Bennett, in their history of the Dissenting interest in England up to the early nineteenth century, have similar remarks about Pearce. When he preached, they said, 'the most careless were attentive, the most prejudiced became favourable, and the coldest felt that, in spite of themselves, they began to kindle.' But it was when he prayed in public, they remarked, that Pearce's spiritual ardour was most apparent. Then the 'most devout were so elevated beyond their former heights, that they said, "We scarcely ever seemed to pray before."'[2] In fact, for some decades after his death it was not uncommon to hear him referred to as the 'seraphic Pearce'.[3]

Formative years, 1766–89

Pearce was born in Plymouth on 20 July 1766, to devout Baptist parents.[4] His mother died when he was but an infant, and so he was raised by his godly father, William Pearce (d. 1805) and an equally pious grandfather. He would also have known the nurturing influence of the 'sturdy Baptist community' of Plymouth, whose history reached back well into the seventeenth century.[5] The heritage of these Baptists is well seen in the character of one of their early ministers, Abraham Cheare (d. 1668).[6]

During the time of the great persecution from 1660 to 1688 of all those Christian bodies outside of the Church of England, Cheare was arrested, cruelly treated and imprisoned on Drake's Island, a small island in Plymouth Sound. Fearful that some of his flock might compromise their Baptist convictions to avoid persecution, he wrote a number of letters to his church during the course of his imprisonment. In one of them he cites with approval a statement from the *Irenicum* (1646) of 'holy Burroughs', that is, the Puritan author Jeremiah Burroughs (*c.*1599–1646). 'I desire to be a faithful Minister of Christ and his Church, if I cannot be a Prudent one,' Cheare quotes from Burroughs' 'Epistle to the Reader', 'standing in the gap is more dangerous and troublesom [*sic*] than getting behind the hedge, there you may be more secure and under the wind; but it's best to be there where God looks for a man'.[7] Cheare himself was one who 'stood in the gap', for he died in 1668 while a prisoner for his Baptist convictions.

As Pearce came into his teen years, however, he consciously spurned the rich heritage of his godly home and the Plymouth Baptist community. According to his own testimony, 'several vicious school-fellows' became his closest friends and he set his heart on what he would later describe as 'evil' and 'wicked inclinations'.[8] But God had better plans for his life. In the summer of 1782, a young preacher by the name of Isaiah Birt (1758–1837) came to preach for a few Sundays in the Plymouth meeting-house.[9] The Spirit of God drove home Birt's words to Pearce's heart. The change in Pearce from what he later called 'a state of death in trespasses and sins' to a 'life in a dear dying Redeemer' was sudden but genuine and lasting.[10] After his conversion Pearce was especially conscious of the Spirit's witness within his heart that he was a child of God and of being 'filled with peace and joy unspeakable'.[11] A year or so later, on the day when he celebrated his seventeenth birthday, he was baptized as a believer and joined the Plymouth congregation in which he had been raised.

It was not long after his baptism that the church perceived that Pearce had been endowed with definite gifts that marked him out as one called to pastoral ministry. So, in November of 1785, when he was only nineteen years of age and serving as an apprentice to his father who was a silversmith, Pearce received a call from the church to engage in the ministry of the Word. The church recommended that Pearce first pursue a course of study at the Bristol Baptist Academy. From August 1786 to May 1789 Pearce thus studied at what was then the sole Baptist institution in Great Britain for the training of ministers for the Calvinistic Baptist denomination. The benefits afforded by this period of study were ones for which Pearce was ever grateful. There was, for example, the privilege of studying under Caleb Evans, the Principal of the Academy, and Robert Hall Jr — the former a key figure in the late eighteenth-century Calvinistic Baptist community and the latter a reputed genius and one who was destined to become one of the great preachers of the early decades of the next century.[12]

Then there were the opportunities for the students to preach and try their wings, as it were. A number of years later Pearce recalled one occasion when he went to preach among the colliers of Coleford, Gloucestershire, the town in which his father in the faith, Isaiah Birt, had grown up. Standing on a three-legged stool in a hut, he directed thirty or forty of these miners to 'the Lamb of God which taketh away the sin of the world'. 'Such an unction from above' attended his preaching that day that the entirety of his hearers were 'melted into tears' and he too, 'weeping among them, could scarcely speak … for interrupting sighs and sobs'.

Finally, there was the rich fellowship to be enjoyed with fellow students. Among the latter, one in particular became a very close friend, William Steadman (1764–1837), later to play a central role in Baptist renewal in the North of England.[13]

Cannon Street Baptist Church, 1789–99

Early in 1789 Pearce received and accepted a call to serve for a year's probation as the pastor of Cannon Street Baptist Church in

Birmingham. He had supplied the Birmingham pulpit the previous summer as well as over the Christmas vacation. Impressed by Pearce's evangelistic zeal — a number were saved on both occasions — along with his ability to edify God's people, the church sent their request to him in early February 1789. Five weeks later Pearce wrote back consenting to their request, and by June, his studies finished, he was with them.[14] The following year he was formally called to be the pastor of what would turn out to be his only pastoral charge. In his letter of acceptance, written on 18 July 1790, he told the Birmingham Baptists that he hoped the union between pastor and church would 'be for God's glory, for the good of precious souls, for your prosperity as a Church, and for my prosperity as your minister'.[15] It is noteworthy that he placed 'God's glory' in first place. If there was any concern that set the fundamental tone for his ministry it was this desire to see God glorified in his life and labours. It is also noteworthy that he asked to be given a yearly holiday of six weeks so that he could visit his father in Plymouth.[16]

His ministry at Cannon Street occupied ten all-too-brief years. Yet they were ones of great fruitfulness. No less than 335 individuals were baptized during his ministry and received into the membership of Cannon Street. This figure does not include those converted under his preaching who, for one reason or another, did not join themselves to the Birmingham cause. A Sunday school was started in 1795 and within a very short period of time grew to the point that some 1200 scholars were enrolled in it.[17]

At the heart of his preaching and spirituality was that key-note of evangelicalism, the mercy of God displayed in the cross of Christ. Writing one Sunday afternoon to William Summers, a friend then residing in London, Pearce told him that he had for his sermon that evening 'the best subject of all in the Bible. Eph. i.7 — Redemption! how welcome to the captive! Forgiveness! how delightful to the guilty! Grace! how pleasant to the heart of a saved

Reflections on the Character and State of departed Christians :

IN

A SERMON,

OCCASIONED BY THE DECEASE

OF

THE REV. CALEB EVANS, D.D.

PASTOR OF THE BAPTIST CONGREGATION, MEETING IN
BROADMEAD, BRISTOL ;

AND SENIOR TUTOR TO THE ACADEMY IN THAT CITY.

Preached in Cannon-street, Birmingham,

SEPTEMBER 4, 1791.

BY SAMUEL PEARCE.

THE MEMORY OF THE JUST IS BLESSED.

BIRMINGHAM,
PRINTED BY J. BELCHER.
SOLD BY T. KNOTT, NO. 47, LOMBARD-STREET, LONDON ;
AND BUTTON, NEWINGTON CAUSEWAY.

1791.

[Price Six-pence.]

Sermon cover: a funeral sermon preached for Caleb
Evans, Principal of Bristol Baptist Academy

sinner!' Christ's atoning death for sinners, he went on to say, is 'the leading truth in the N.T. ... a doctrine I cannot but venerate; and to the Author of such a redemption my whole soul labours to exhaust itself in praise'.[18] And in his final letter to his congregation, written on 31 May 1799, he reminded them that the gospel which he had preached among them for ten years and in which he urged them to stand fast was 'the gospel of the grace of God; the gospel of free, full, everlasting salvation, founded on the sufferings and death of God manifest in the flesh'.[19]

Men and women called him the 'silver-tongued' because of the intensity and power of his preaching.[20] But there were times when preaching was a real struggle for him. Writing to William Carey in 1796, for example, he told the Baptist missionary who at that time was living in Mudnabati, West Bengal:

> *At some times, I question whether I ever knew the grace of God in truth; and at others I hesitate on the most important points of Christian faith. I have lately had peculiar struggles of this kind with my own heart, and have often half concluded to speak no more in the name of the Lord. When I am preparing for the pulpit, I fear I am going to avow fables for facts and doctrines of men for the truths of God. In conversation I am obliged to be silent, lest my tongue should belie my heart. In prayer I know not what to say, and at times think prayer altogether useless. Yet I cannot wholly surrender my hope, or my profession.—Three things I find, above all others, tend to my preservation:—First, a recollection of time when, at once, I was brought to abandon the practice of sins which the fear of damnation could never bring me to relinquish before. Surely, I say, this must be the finger of God, according to the Scripture doctrine of regeneration:—Second, I feel such a consciousness of guilt that nothing but the gospel scheme can satisfy my mind respecting the hope of salvation: and, Thirdly, I see that*

what true devotion does appear in the world, seems only to be found among those to whom Christ is precious.[21]

A handful of his sermons were published, as well as the circular letter for the Midland Baptist Association that he drew up in 1795 and that was entitled *Doctrine of Salvation by Free Grace Alone*. A good perspective on his thought may be found in the following extract from this circular letter:

The point of difference between us and many other professing Christians lies in the doctrine of salvation entirely by grace. For whilst some assert that good works are the cause of justification; some that good works are united with the merits of Christ and so both contribute to our justification; and others that good works neither in whole nor in part justify, but the act of faith; we renounce everything in point of our acceptance with God, but his free Grace alone which justifies the ungodly, still treading in the steps of our venerable forefathers, the compilers of the Baptist Confession of Faith, who thus express themselves respecting the doctrine of justification: 'Those whom God effectually calleth, he also freely justifieth … for Christ's sake alone; not by imputing faith itself, the act of believing, or any other evangelical obedience to them as their righteousness; but by imputing Christ's active obedience unto the whole law, and passive obedience in his death for their whole and sole righteousness, they receiving and resting on him and his righteousness by faith' which 'is the alone instrument of justification'.[22]

In this point do all the other lines of our confession meet. For if it be admitted that justification is an act of free grace in God without any respect to the merit or demerit of the person justified, then the doctrines of Jehovah's sovereign love in choosing to himself a people from before the foundation of the world, his sending his Son to expiate their guilt, his effectual operations upon their hearts, and his perfecting the work he has begun in them until those whom he justifies he also glorifies, will be embraced as necessary parts of the glorious scheme of our salvation.[23]

Sarah Pearce

A vital support to Pearce throughout his pastorate at Cannon Street was his closest friend, his wife Sarah Hopkins (1771–1804). A third-generation Baptist,[24] Sarah had met Pearce soon after his arrival in Birmingham. Pearce was soon deeply in love with Sarah and she with him. As he wrote to her on 24 December 1790, about the impact her letters had on him:

> *Were I averse to writing … one of your dear Epistles could not fail of conquering the antipathy and transforming it into desire. The moment I peruse a line from my Sarah, I am inspired at the propensity which never leaves me, till I have thrown open my whole heart, and returned a copy of it to the dear being who long since compelled it to a voluntary surrender, and whose claims have never since been disputed.*[25]

They were married on 2 February 1791. Pearce's understanding of what should lie at the heart of their marriage finds expression in a letter that he wrote to his future wife a little over two months before their wedding: 'may my dear Sarah & myself be made the means of leading each other on in the way to the heavenly kingdom & at last there meet to know what even temporary separation means no more'.[26]

Pearce's love for his wife clearly deepened with the passing of the years. Three and a half years after their marriage, he wrote to her from Plymouth: 'O, my Sarah, had I as much proof of my love to Christ as I have of my love to you, I should prize it above rubies.'[27] And when Pearce was away from his wife the following year, 1795, on a preaching trip in London, he wrote to tell her that 'every day improves not only my tenderness but my *esteem* for you'. On the same trip he called her 'the dearest of women — my invaluable Sarah'.[28] In another letter written about the same time he informed the one whom he called the 'partner of my heart' that his letter was a 'forerunner of her impatient husband who weary with so long an absence' — he had obviously been away from home for a few weeks — '[longs] again to embrace his dearest friend'.[29]

The following year, when he was involved in an extensive preaching trip in Ireland, he wrote to his wife from Dublin on 24 June 1796: 'last evening … were my eyes delighted at the sight of a letter from my dear Sarah … I rejoice that you, as well as myself, find that "absence diminishes not affection". For my part I compare our present correspondence to a kind of courtship, rendered sweeter than what usually bears that name by a *certainty of success* … Not less than when I sought your hand [in marriage], do I now court your heart, nor doth the *security* of possessing you at all lessen my pleasure at the prospect of calling you my own, when we meet again.' And then towards the end of the letter he added: 'O our dear fireside! When shall we sit down toe to toe, and tete á [*sic*] tete again — Not a long time I hope will elapse ere I re-enjoy that felicity.'[30]

That Sarah felt the same towards Samuel is seen in a letter she wrote after her husband's death to her sister Rebecca. Rebecca had just been married to a Mr Harris and Sarah prayed that she might 'enjoy the most uninterrupted Happiness … (for indeed I can scarce form an idia [*sic*] … this side of Heaven of greater) equal to what I *have* enjoyed'.[31]

One final word about Samuel and Sarah's marriage needs to be said. What especially delighted Pearce about his wife was her passion for God. As he told her in the summer of 1793 in response to a letter he had received from her: 'I cannot convey to you an Idea of the holy rapture I felt at the account you gave me of your soul prosperity.'[32]

An evangelistic piety

One leading characteristic of Pearce's spirituality has already been noted, namely, its crucicentrism. 'Christ crucified,' his good friend Andrew Fuller (1754-1815) wrote of him, 'was his darling theme, from first to last'.[33]

A second prominent feature of his spirituality was a passion for the salvation of his fellow human beings. On a preaching trip to Wales, for instance, he wrote to Sarah about the lovely countryside that he was passing through: 'every pleasant scene which opened to us on our way (& they were very numerous) lost half its beauty because my lovely Sarah was not present to partake its pleasures with me.' But, he added, 'to see the Country was not the immediate object of my visiting Wales — I came to preach the gospel — to tell poor Sinners of the dear Lord Jesus — to endeavour to restore the children of misery to the pious pleasures of divine enjoyment'.[34]

This passion is strikingly revealed in three events.

Preaching at Guilsborough

The first took place when he was asked to preach at the opening of a Baptist meeting-house in Guilsborough, Northamptonshire, in May 1794. The previous meeting-house had been burnt down at Christmas 1792, by a mob that was hostile to Baptists. Pearce had spoken in the morning on Psalm 76:10 ('Surely the wrath of man shall praise thee: the remainder of wrath shalt thou restrain'). Later that day, during the midday meal, it was quite evident from the conversation that was going at the dinner tables that Pearce's sermon had been warmly appreciated. It was thus no surprise when Pearce was asked if he would be willing to preach again the following morning. 'If you will find a congregation,' Pearce responded, 'I will find a sermon.' It was agreed to have the sermon at 5.00 a.m. so that a number of farm labourers could come who wanted to hear Pearce preach and who would have to be at their tasks early in the morning.

After Pearce had preached the second time, and that to a congregation of more than 200 people, and he was sitting at breakfast with a few others, including Andrew Fuller, the latter remarked to Pearce how pleased he had been with the content of his friend's sermon. But, he went on to say, it seemed to him that Pearce's sermon was poorly structured. 'I thought,' Fuller told his friend, 'you did not seem to close when you had really finished. I wondered that, contrary to what is usual with you, you seemed, as it were, to begin again at the end — how was it?' Pearce's response was terse: 'It was so; but I had my reason.' 'Well then, come, let us have it,' Fuller jovially responded. Pearce was quite reluctant to divulge the reason, but after a further entreaty from Fuller, he consented and said:

> Well, my brother, you shall have the secret, if it must be so. Just at the moment I was about to resume my seat, thinking I had finished, the door opened, and I saw a poor man enter, of the working class; and from the sweat on his brow, and the symptoms of his fatigue, I conjectured that he had walked some miles to this early service, but that he had been unable to reach the place till the close. A momentary thought glanced through my mind — here may be a man who never heard

*the gospel, or it may be he is one that regards it as a feast
of fat things; in either case, the effort on his part demands
one on mine. So with the hope of doing him good, I resolved
at once to forget all else, and, in despite of criticism, and the
apprehension of being thought tedious, to give him a quarter
of an hour.*[35]

As Fuller and the others present at the breakfast table listened to this
simple explanation, they were deeply impressed by Pearce's evident
love for souls. Not afraid to appear as one lacking in homiletical
skill, especially in the eyes of his fellow pastors, Pearce's zeal for the
spiritual health of *all* his hearers had led him to minister as best he
could to this 'poor man' who had arrived late.

'Establishing the empire of my dear Lord'

Given his ardour for the advance of the gospel it is only to be expected
that Pearce would be vitally involved in the formation in October
1792 of what would eventually be termed the Baptist Missionary
Society, the womb of the modern missionary movement. In fact,
by 1794 Pearce was so deeply gripped by the cause of missions that
he had arrived at the conviction that he should offer his services to
the society and go out to India to join the first missionary team the
society had sent out, namely, William Carey, John Thomas (1757–
1801), and their respective families. He began to study Bengali
on his own.[36] And for the entire month of October 1794, which
preceded the early November meeting of the society's administrative
committee where Pearce's offer would be evaluated, Pearce set apart
'one day in every week to secret prayer and fasting' for direction.[37]
He also kept a diary of his experiences during this period, much
of which Fuller later inserted verbatim into his *Memoirs* of Pearce
and which admirably displays what Fuller described as his friend's
'singular submissiveness to the will of God'.[38]

During one of these days of prayer, fasting, and seeking God's face, Pearce recorded how God met with him in a remarkable way. Pearce had begun the day with 'solemn prayer for the assistance of the Holy Spirit' so that he might 'enjoy the spirit and power of prayer,' have his 'personal religion improved', and his 'public steps directed'. He proceeded to read a portion of Jonathan Edwards' life of the American missionary David Brainerd, a book that quickened the zeal of many of Pearce's generation, and to peruse 2 Corinthians 2–6. Afterwards he went to prayer, but, he recorded, his heart was hard and 'all was dullness', and he feared that somehow he had offended God.

Suddenly, Pearce wrote, 'it pleased God to smite the rock with the rod of his Spirit, and immediately the waters began to flow.' Likening the frame of his heart to the rock in the desert that Moses struck with his rod in order to bring forth water from it (see Exodus 17:1-6), Pearce had found himself unable to generate any profound warmth for God and his dear cause. God, as it were, had to come by his Spirit, 'touch' Pearce's heart and so quicken his affections. He was overwhelmed, he wrote, by 'a heavenly glorious melting power'. He saw afresh 'the love of a crucified Redeemer' and 'the attractions of his cross'. He felt 'like Mary [Madgalene] at the master's feet weeping, for tenderness of soul; like a little child, for submission to my heavenly father's will'. The need to take the gospel to those who had never heard it gripped him anew 'with an irresistible drawing of soul' and, in his own words, 'compelled me to vow that I would, by his leave, serve him among the heathen'. As he wrote later in his diary:

> *If ever in my life I knew any thing of the influences of the Holy Spirit, I did at this time. I was swallowed up in God. Hunger, fulness, cold, heat, friends and enemies, all seemed nothing before God. I was in a new world. All was delightful; for Christ was all, and in all. Many times I concluded prayer, but when*

rising from my knees, communion with God was so desirable,
that I was sweetly drawn to it again and again, till my ...
strength was almost exhausted.[39]

The decision of the society as to Pearce's status was ultimately a
negative one. When the executive committee of the society met at
Roade, Northamptonshire, on 12 November, it was of the opinion
that Pearce could best serve the cause of missions at home in
England. Pearce's response to this decision is best seen in extracts
from two letters. The first, written to his wife Sarah the day after he
received the decision, stated: 'I am disappointed, but not dismayed.
I ever wish to make my Saviour's will my own.'[40] The second, sent to
William Carey over four months later, contains a similar desire to
submit to the perfectly good and sovereign will of God.

Instead of a letter, you perhaps expected to have seen the
writer; and had the will of God been so, he would by this time
have been on his way to Mudnabatty: but it is not in man
that walketh to direct his steps. Full of hope and expectation
as I was, when I wrote you last, that I should be honoured
with a mission to the poor heathen, and be an instrument
of establishing the empire of my dear Lord in India, I must
submit now to stand still, and see the salvation of God.

Pearce then told Carey some of the details of the November
meeting at which the society executive had made their decision
regarding his going overseas.

I shall ever love my dear brethren the more for the tenderness
with which they treated me, and the solemn prayer they
repeatedly put up to God for me. At last, I withdrew for them
to decide, and whilst I was apart from them, and engaged in
prayer for divine direction, I felt all anxiety forsake me, and an
entire resignation of will to the will of God, be it what it would,

together with a satisfaction that so much praying breath would not be lost; but that He who hath promised to be found of all that seek him, would assuredly direct the hearts of my brethren to that which was most pleasing to himself, and most suitable to the interests of his kingdom in the world. Between two and three hours were they deliberating after which time a paper was put into my hands, of which the following is a copy.

'The brethren at this meeting are fully satisfied of the fitness of brother P[earce]'s qualifications, and greatly approve of the disinterestedness of his motives and the ardour of his mind. But another Missionary not having been requested, and not being in our view immediately necessary, and brother P[earce] occupying already a post very important to the prosperity of the Mission itself, we are unanimously of opinion that at present, however, he should continue in the situation which he now occupies.'

In response to this decision, which dashed some of Pearce's deepest longings, he was, he said, 'enabled cheerfully to reply, "The will of the Lord be done"; and receiving this answer as the voice of God, I have, for the most part, been easy since, though not without occasional pantings of spirit after the publishing of the gospel to the Pagans'.[41]

From the vantage-point of the highly individualistic spirit of twenty-first-century Western Christianity, Pearce's friends seem to have been quite wrong in refusing to send him to India. If, during his month of fasting and prayer, he had felt he knew God's will for his life, was not the Baptist Missionary Society executive wrong in the decision they made? And should not Pearce have persisted in pressing his case for going? While these questions may seem natural ones to ask given the cultural matrix of contemporary Western Christianity, Pearce knew himself to be part of a team and he was more interested in the triumph of that team's strategy than the fulfilment of his own personal desires.[42]

Praying for the French

In the three remaining years of Pearce's earthly life, he expended much of his energy in raising support for the cause of foreign missions. As he informed Carey in the fall of 1797:

I can hardly refrain from repeating what I have so often told you before, that I long to meet you on earth and to join you in your labours of love among the poor dear heathens. Yes, would my Lord bid me so, I should with transport obey the summons and take a joyful farewell of the land that bare me, though it were for ever. But I must confess that the path of duty appears to me clearer than before to be at home, at least for the present. Not that I think my connexions in England a sufficient argument, but that I am somewhat necessary to the Mission itself, and shall be as long as money is wanted and our number of active friends does not increase. Brother Fuller and myself have the whole of the collecting business on our hands, and though there are many others about us who exceed me in grace and gifts, yet their other engagements forbid or their peculiar turn of mind disqualifies them for that kind of service. I wish, however, to be thankful if our dear Lord will but employ me as a foot in the body. I consider myself as united to the hands and eyes, and mouth, and heart, and all; and when the body rejoices, I have my share of gladness with the other members.[43]

One of the meetings at which Pearce preached was the one that saw William Ward — later to be one of the most invaluable of Carey's co-workers in India — accepted as a missionary with the Baptist

Missionary Society. Those attending the meeting, which took place at Kettering on 16 October 1798, were deeply stirred by Pearce's passion and concern for the advance of the gospel. He preached 'like an Apostle', Fuller later wrote to Carey. And when Ward wrote to Carey, he told his future colleague that Pearce 'set the whole meeting in a flame. Had missionaries been needed, we might have had a cargo immediately'.[44]

Returning back to Birmingham from this meeting Pearce was caught in a heavy downpour of rain, drenched to the skin, and subsequently developed a severe chill. Neglecting to rest and foolishly thinking what he called 'pulpit sweats' would effect a cure, he continued a rigorous schedule of preaching at Cannon Street as well as in outlying villages around Birmingham. His lungs became so inflamed that Pearce was necessitated to ask Ward to supply the Cannon Street pulpit for a few months during the winter of 1798–99. As Pearce wrote Ward in a letter:

> *Do you want time? You shall have it here. Do you want books? You shall have them here. Do you want a friend? Be assured, the hand, that moves this pen, belongs to a heart warmly attached to you. If you love me — come and help me. Come and secure the hearts and prayers of the hundreds of Birmingham Christians, who only want to know you, to love you too.*[45]

Pearce and Ward appear to have thought that this arrangement would be for only a few weeks. As it was, Ward ended up staying for three months, from mid-December 1798 to the beginning of March 1799.[46] The two men developed a deep friendship, as Ward later told Pearce, 'your name, your virtues are engraven on my heart in indelible characters'.[47]

By mid-December 1798 Pearce could not converse for more than a few minutes without losing his breath. Yet still he was thinking of the salvation of the lost. Writing to Carey around this time, he told him of a plan to take the gospel to France that he had been mulling over in his mind. Great Britain and France were locked in a titanic war, the Napoleonic War, which would last into the middle of the second decade of the next century. This war was the final and climactic episode in a struggle that had dominated the eighteenth century. Not surprisingly, there was little love lost between the British and the French. Samuel Carter Hall (1800–89), an English literary figure, for example, recalled one of his earliest memories as a young boy when his father would put him on his knee and tell him, 'Be a good boy, love your mother, and hate the French'![48]

But Pearce was gripped by a far different passion than those that gripped many in Britain and France — his was the priority of the kingdom of Christ. In one of the last sermons that he ever preached, on a day of public thanksgiving for Horatio Nelson's annihilation of the French Fleet at the Battle of the Nile (1798) and the repulse of a French invasion fleet off the coast of Ireland in the fall of 1799, Pearce pointedly said:

> *Should any one expect that I shall introduce the* destruction *of our foes, by the late victories gained off the coasts of Egypt and Ireland, as the object of pleasure and gratitude, he will be disappointed. The man who can take pleasure at the destruction of his fellow men, is a cannibal at heart … but to the heart of him who calls himself a disciple of the merciful Jesus, let such pleasure be an everlasting stranger. Since in that sacred volume, which I revere as the fair gift of heaven to man, I am taught, that 'of one blood God hath made all nations', [Acts 17:26] it is impossible for me not to regard every man as my brother, and to consider, that national differences ought not to excite personal animosities.*[49]

A few months later — when he was desperately ill — he wrote a letter to Carey telling him of his plans for a missionary journey to France. 'I have been endeavouring for some years,' he told Carey, 'to get five of our Ministers to agree that they will apply themselves to the French language … then we [for he was obviously intending to be one of the five] might spend two months annually in that Country, and at least satisfy ourselves that Christianity was not lost in France for want of a fair experiment in its favour: and who can tell what God might do!'[50] God would use British evangelicals, notably Pearce's Baptist contemporary Robert Haldane (1764–1842), to take the gospel to Francophones on the Continent when peace eventually came, but Pearce's anointed preaching would play no part in that great work. Yet his ardent prayers on behalf of the French could not have been without some effect. As Pearce had noted in 1794 'praying breath' is never lost.

The 'religion for a dying sinner'

By the spring of 1799 Pearce was desperately ill with pulmonary tuberculosis. Leaving his wife and family — he and Sarah had five children by this time — he went to the south of England from April to July in the hope that rest there might effect a cure. Being away from his wife and children, though, only aggravated his suffering. Writing to Sarah — 'the dear object of my tenderest, my warmest love' — from Plymouth, he requested her to 'write me as soon as you receive this' and signed it 'ever, ever, ever, wholly yours'. Three weeks later when he wrote, he sent Sarah 'a thousand & 10 thousand thousand embraces', and then poignantly added, 'may the Lord hear our daily prayers for each other!'[51]

Sarah and the children had gone to stay with her family in Alcester, twenty or miles or so from Birmingham. But by mid-May Sarah could no longer bear being absent from her beloved. Leaving their children with Birmingham friends, she headed south, where she stayed with her husband until the couple slowly made their way home to Birmingham in mid-July.[52] By this time Samuel's voice was so far gone that he could not even whisper without pain in his lungs. His suffering, though, seemed to act like a refiner's fire to draw him closer to Christ. 'Blessed be his dear name,' he said not long before his death, 'who shed his blood for me … Now I see the value of the religion of the cross. It is a religion for a dying sinner … Yes, I taste its sweetness, and enjoy its fulness, with all the gloom of a dying-bed before me; and far rather would I be the poor emaciated and emaciating creature that I am, than be an emperor with every earthly good about him, but without a God.'[53] Some of his final words were for Sarah: 'I trust our separation will not be forever … we shall meet again.'[54]

He fell asleep in Christ on Thursday 10 October 1799. William Ward, who had been profoundly influenced by Pearce's zeal and spirituality, well summed up his character when he wrote not long before the latter's death: 'Oh, how does personal religion shine in Pearce! What a soul! What ardour for the glory of God! … you see in him a mind wholly given up to God; a sacred lustre shines in his conversation: always tranquil, always cheerful … I have seen more of God in him than in any other person I ever met.'[55]

William Carey (1761–1834) and his pundit Mrityunjaya

7

'A wretched, poor
and helpless worm':

Revival activism: the legacy of William Carey[1]

For English-speaking people, the eighteenth century was an era of highly significant achievements. Through conquest and exploration, for instance, they established themselves as the masters of a far-flung empire that encircled the globe. It was in the middle of this century that British troops under the command of Robert Clive (1725–74) defeated a French army in India at the Battle of Plassey, which paved the way for the British conquest of Bengal and later all of India. Two years later on 13 September 1759, General James Wolfe (1727–59) defeated the French General Louis Joseph Montcalm (1712–59) at the Battle of the Plains of Abraham, then outside the walls of the city of Quebec. Though Wolfe was killed in this engagement, the British victory meant the end of French rule in Canada. Ten or so years later, Captain James Cook (1728–79), a British naval officer, entered upon his world-changing expeditions in the South Pacific, discovering and mapping the coastlines of New Zealand and Australia.

Running parallel to this empire-building by the British, though initially quite distinct from it, came the kingdom-building by

English-speaking missionaries. Up until the latter part of the eighteenth century, Evangelical Christianity was primarily confined to northern Europe and the Atlantic seaboard of North America. But suddenly in the last decade of the century Evangelicals launched out from these two geographical regions and began to establish churches throughout Asia, Africa and Australasia. At the heart of this missionary movement was the man that we want to look at in this chapter: William Carey. His ministry and legacy were, it needs emphasizing, the very fruit of the revival that we have been thinking about in this book.[2]

'Such a man as Carey is more to me than bishop or archbishop: he is an apostle.' This was the estimate that the Evangelical Anglican John Newton once expressed about the Baptist missionary William Carey. On another occasion, Newton wrote that he did not look for miracles in his own day on the order of those done in the Apostolic era, yet, he went on, 'if God were to work one in our day, I should not wonder if it were in favour of Dr. Carey.'[3] And when in 1826, two missionaries by the names of George Bennet and Daniel Tyerman happened to visit Carey in India (by that time he had been labouring there over thirty years), they commented on his 'apostolic appearance.'[4]

Carey's opinion of himself was quite different, however. Like others who have seen something of the holiness and glory of God in the light of revival, he knew himself to be anything but a holy man. As he told his son Jabez in 1831: 'My direct and positive sins are innumerable; my negligence in the Lord's work has been great; I have not promoted his cause nor sought his glory and honour as I ought.'[5] When he came to die in 1834, he thus gave explicit instructions that on his tombstone were to be placed the following words drawn from a hymn by Isaac Watts (1674–1748):

A wretched, poor, and helpless worm,
On Thy kind arms I fall.

Carey and his close colleagues, Joshua Marshman and William Ward, were quite conscious that they did not merit being decked out with halos like medieval saints, something that the later Baptist and Evangelical tradition — following Newton's lead? — has done, at least with respect to Carey. Each of these men was convinced that he had simply done his duty as a servant of Christ.[6] For Carey that duty had begun about fifty-five years before when he fled to Christ for 'strength and righteousness'.

Early influences

Carey was born of poor parents in 1761 in a tiny village called Paulerspury in the heart of Northamptonshire. Carey's parents were staunch Anglicans. His father, Edmund (d. 1816), the schoolmaster of Paulerspury, was what was known as the Parish Clerk. According to William Cowper, the Evangelical hymnwriter and close friend of John Newton, the Parish Clerk had to 'pronounce the amen to prayers and announce the sermon', lead the chants and the responses during the church service, keep the church register of baptisms, marriages, and burials, and chase 'dogs out of church and force … unwilling youngsters in'.[7] Thus, young William was regularly taken to church. Of this early acquaintance with the Church of England, Carey later wrote:

> *Having been accustomed from my infancy to read the Scriptures, I had a considerable acquaintance therewith, especially with the historical parts. I … have no doubt but the constant reading of the Psalms, Lessons, etc. in the parish church, which I was obliged to attend regularly, tended to furnish my mind with a general Scripture knowledge. [But] of real experimental religion I scarcely heard anything till I was fourteen years of age.*[8]

Also living in Paulerspury was William's uncle, Peter Carey. Peter had served with General James Wolfe in Canada during the French and Indian War (aka the Seven Years' War), and had seen action at the British capture of the citadel of Quebec in 1759, two years before William was born. Peter subsequently returned to England, and worked in Paulerspury as a gardener. His tales of Canada almost certainly awakened in young William an unquenchable interest in far-off lands.

Moreover, Peter implanted in young William a love of gardens and flowers that remained with him all of his life. His younger sister Mary later recalled:

> *He often took me over the dirtiest roads to get at a plant or an insect. He never walked out, I think … without observation on the hedges as he passed; and when he took up a plant of any kind he always observed it with care.*[9]

This passion for botany was not diminished one whit by the passage of time. When, years later, Carey was established in India, he was continually asking his friends and correspondents to send him seeds, roots and bulbs. For instance, in a letter to his close friend John Sutcliff, he asked him to send him 'a few tulips, daffodils, snowdrops, lilies'. When Sutcliff dragged his feet about collecting them, Carey chided him: 'Were you to give a boy a penny a day to gather seeds of cowslips, violets, daisies, crowfoots, etc., and to dig up the roots of bluebells, after they have flowered, you might fill me a box each quarter. My American friends are twenty times more communicative in this respect than my English. Do try to mend a little.'[10]

In fact, at Serampore in India, Carey had five acres of garden under cultivation. Cultivating this garden served as a welcome means of relaxation amid the stresses and strains of ministry in India. It was of this garden that his son Jonathan later remarked that 'here he [i.e., his father] enjoyed his most pleasant moments of secret meditation and devotion'.[11] Carey's gardening activities

118

in India would ultimately lead to the formation of a horticultural society, which helped to introduce agricultural reform to Bengal, where Carey was ministering. These reforms would do much to alleviate the plight of the Bengali who suffered greatly owing to the backward state of their agriculture.[12]

Conversion

So much did young Carey love gardening that he wanted to become a gardener like his uncle Peter. At this point in his life, however, Carey suffered from a skin disease that made it very painful for him to spend large amounts of time in the full sun. And so, in his mid-teens, his father apprenticed him to a shoemaker by the name of Clarke Nichols who lived in Piddington, about seven miles away from his home. This apprenticeship was to have very significant consequences for William, for one of his fellow apprentices was a Christian. His name was John Warr; he was a Congregationalist and was used of God to bring Carey to Christ. It was known for a long time that Carey's salvation had come partly as the result of the witness of one of his fellow apprentices. Until the First World War, however, the name of this apprentice had been completely lost. During that war it was found in a letter of Carey's which had only then come to light. It is a powerful illustration of how the faithful witness of one believer can have immense significance.

At first, when Warr shared his faith with Carey, Carey resisted. It is vital to recall that he was the product of a staunch Anglican home and that he had learned to look down on, indeed despise, anyone who was not an Anglican. John lent him books and then invited him to attend on a regular basis the mid-week gathering of Congregationalists in Hackleton, a nearby village, for prayer and Bible study. Carey went and came under deep conviction. He tried to reform his life: to give up lying and swearing, and to take up prayer. But at this point in his life he did not realize that a definite change in his lifestyle in this regard could only occur when he had been given, in the language of Scripture, a new heart.

Coupled with Warr's testimony was an important lesson that young Carey learned from a traumatic incident that took place at Christmas 1777. It was the custom for apprentices at that time of the year to be given small amounts of money from the trades-people with whom their masters had business. Carey had had to go to Northampton to make some purchases for his master as well as for himself. At one particular shop, that of an ironmonger called Hall, he was personally given a counterfeit shilling as a joke. When Carey discovered the worthless coin he decided, not without some qualms of conscience, to pass it off to his employer. Appropriating a good shilling from the money that Nichols had given him, he included the counterfeit shilling among the change for his master. On the way back to Piddington, he even prayed that if God enabled his dishonesty to go undetected he would break with sin from that time forth!

But, Carey commented many years later, 'a gracious God did not get me through'.[13] Carey's dishonesty was discovered, he was covered with shame and disgrace, and became afraid to go out in the village where he lived for fear of what others were thinking about him. By this means, Carey was led, he subsequently said, to 'see much more of myself than I had ever done before, and to seek for mercy with greater earnestness'.[14] That mercy he found as over the next two years he came to 'depend on a crucified Saviour for pardon and salvation'.[15]

Baptist convictions

Carey continued to go with Warr to the prayer-meetings in Hackleton, but it was not until 10 February 1779 that he actually attended a worship service. On that particular day a man named Thomas Chater (d. 1811), a resident of Olney, was preaching. The text on which Chater was preaching has not been recorded, but in his sermon he did quote that powerful exhortation in Hebrews 13:13: 'Let us go forth therefore unto him [i.e. Jesus] without the camp, bearing his reproach.' On the basis of this verse Chater urged upon his hearers 'the necessity of following Christ entirely'. As Carey listened to Chater's exhortation, the interpretation that he made of this text and Chater's words was one that he would later describe as 'very crude'. He distinctly felt that God was calling him to leave the Church of England, where, in his particular parish church, he was sitting under 'a lifeless, carnal ministry', and to unite with a Dissenting congregation. Since the Church of England was established by the law of the land, he reasoned, its members were 'protected from the scandal of the cross'.[16] So Carey became what he had long despised — a Dissenter.

During the first few years after his conversion, Carey struggled 'to crystallize his beliefs, to establish foundations on which to build his faith'.[17] 'Having so slight an acquaintance with ministers,' he later wrote, 'I was obliged to draw all from the Bible alone.'[18] His study of the Scriptures soon led him to the realization that infant-baptism, as practised by Anglicans and Congregationalists, had no real scriptural authority behind it. Thus, in the course of 1783, he approached John Ryland Sr, pastor of College Lane Baptist Church in Northampton, for baptism. Ryland Sr in turn asked his son, John Ryland Jr, to baptize Carey. So it was that in the early hours of 5 October 1785 the younger Ryland baptized Carey in the River Nene that then flowed through Northampton. Obviously at the time, neither of these two men realized what the future would hold, and how they would become firm friends and co-labourers in a great work of God.

A growing passions for missions

Around the time of his baptism Carey came across the accounts of the voyages of discovery undertaken by James Cook in the Pacific. Iain H. Murray has rightly observed that 'the end of Cook's geographical feat [was] the beginning of missionary enterprise'.[19] Carey would later say regarding his perusal of these volumes: 'Reading Cook's voyages was the first thing that engaged my mind to think of missions.'[20] Through these accounts, Carey's boyhood desire to know about other lands was given substance and shape. More importantly, through the written account of Cook's voyages, Carey began to gaze upon wider spiritual horizons than the fields of Northamptonshire, and to reflect on the desperate spiritual plight of those who lived in the countries that Cook had discovered. Many of them had no written language, certainly none of them had the Scriptures in their own tongues, and there were neither local churches nor resident ministers to share with them the good news of God's salvation. 'Pity, therefore, humanity, and much more Christianity,' he wrote only a few years after reading Cook's journals, called 'loudly for every possible exertion to introduce the gospel amongst them.'[21] Between 1785 and 1793 one of Carey's main preoccupations became the collection of information, especially geographical and religious, about the many other nations of the world that had never heard a word of the gospel.

Carey's growing passion for the evangelization of nations outside of Europe did not cause him to forget the need of the many at his own backdoor. Through his witness, for example, his two sisters, Mary and Ann, were won to Christ. As is often the case with the members of one's own family, William had not found it at all easy to speak to them concerning their need of Christ. However, he persevered in praying for them, and when Mary Carey thought back on this period of her life, she could only exclaim, 'O what a privilege to have praying relations, and what a mercy to have a God that waits to be gracious!'[22] The two sisters were baptized in 1783.

Preaching and pastoral ministry in England

By the time that his sisters were baptized, Carey had begun

preaching. He first preached at the church in Hackleton. He then began speaking in the village of Moulton, Northamptonshire, where he was called to be pastor in 1785. Finally, the ministry took him to Leicester, where he was pastor of Harvey Lane Baptist Church from 1789 to 1793, and from whence Carey set sail for India. His formal ordination occurred on 1 August 1787 in the village of Moulton.

Taking part in his ordination were three Baptist pastors who would become his life-long friends and who would be the pillars of the missionary society which sent him to India, that is, the Baptist Missionary Society: John Ryland Jr, Andrew Fuller, and John Sutcliff, pastor of Olney Baptist Church, where Carey had his membership for a couple of years. It is quite misleading to suppose that it was Carey's single-handed effort that brought about the founding of the Baptist Missionary Society and enabled him to accomplish all that he did in India from 1793 till his death over forty years later. As we have seen, Carey was part of a close-knit circle of like-minded friends, without whom little of what he longed for would have been realized. As Scottish Baptist Christopher Anderson maintained during Carey's lifetime, it was the 'strong personal attachment' of these friends to one another that lay behind the 'usefulness' of the Baptist Missionary Society: Carey, Marshman and Ward in India; Sutcliff, Fuller, Ryland and Pearce, at home.[23]

The Enquiry (1792) and its background

Carey's pastorates at Moulton and Leicester admitted him to meeting periodically with other Baptist ministers who pastored churches in what was called the Northamptonshire Baptist Association. This association provided a forum for the exchange of ideas, a meeting place for fellowship as well as mutual spiritual encouragement. At a meeting of the pastors of the association on 30 September 1785,

John Ryland Sr, who was one of the most colourful characters of the eighteenth-century English Baptist community and one of the senior pastors of that body,[24] asked Carey to propose a topic that they could discuss that day. Carey suggested a question that had been running through his mind for some time: 'Whether the command given to the apostles to teach all nations was not binding on all succeeding ministers, to the end of the world, seeing that the accompanying promise was of equal extent.'

Carey's question obviously grew out of meditation upon Matthew 28:18-20. If, Carey reasoned, Christ's promise of his presence with his people is for all time (v. 20), what then of his command to 'teach all nations' about Christ (v. 19a)? Was it not a requirement for the church till the end of history as we know it? Nor would it have escaped Carey's notice that this text was also a traditional passage Baptists had employed in their defence of believer's baptism. In other words, Carey was also implicitly asking: If this command to baptize only believers was of ongoing validity — and the English Baptist community in his day would have wholeheartedly answered this question in the affirmative — what then of the command to evangelize the nations?

According to another pastor who was actually present at this meeting of the Northamptonshire Association ministers, John Webster Morris (1763–1836), then pastor of Clipston Baptist Church in Northamptonshire, Ryland responded with some vehemence to Carey's suggestion and bluntly told the young pastor:

You are a miserable enthusiast for asking such a question. Certainly nothing can be done before another Pentecost, when an effusion of miraculous gifts, including the gift of tongues, will give effect to the commission of Christ as at first. What, Sir! Can you preach in Arabic, in Persic, in Hindustani, in Bengali, that you think it your duty to send the gospel to the heathens?

John C. Marshman (1794–1877), the son of Joshua Marshman, one of Carey's respected co-workers in India, had a similar report about the words of the elder Ryland. As the younger Marshman reported the incident, Ryland apparently dismissed the proposed topic with a frown and told Carey: 'Young man, sit down. When God pleases to convert the heathen, he will do it without your aid or mine!' On the other hand, John Ryland Jr, the son of the elder Ryland, strongly asserted that his father never uttered such sentiments. The burden of proof, however, does seem to indicate that Carey did indeed receive some sort of stinging rebuke from the elder Ryland. Now, the standard interpretation of the elder Ryland's reasoning has been to trace it back to the influence of Hyper-Calvinism.[25] I personally doubt that this is a sufficient theological explanation of Ryland's outburst,[26] though, as we have seen in previous chapters, there is little doubt that Hyper-Calvinism was a major challenge with which Carey and his circle of Baptist friends had to contend.

When Carey came to draw up a written defence of cross-cultural missions, he noted that some of his contemporaries had argued that the command to make disciples from all the nations was no longer incumbent upon the church. The Ancient Church, they maintained, had actually fulfilled that command. Moreover, according to Carey, they argued thus: 'we have enough to do to attend to the salvation of our own countrymen; and that, if God intends the salvation of the heathen, he will some way or other bring them to the gospel, or the gospel to them.'[27]

Carey's response ran in at least three channels — prayer, preaching and printing. First, if souls were to be saved, prayer — persistent, corporate prayer — was vital and all-essential. In the diary of the younger Ryland we thus read:

Brethren, Fuller, Sutcliff, Carey, and I, kept this day as a private fast in my study: read the Epistles to Timothy and Titus ...

and each prayed twice — Carey with singular enlargement and pungency. Our chief design was to implore a revival of the power of godliness in our own souls, in our churches, and in the church at large.[28]

Then, Carey's preaching manifested his concern for the lost. Carey's sermon at a meeting of the Northamptonshire Baptist Association in May 1792 is an excellent example in this regard. Based on Isaiah 54:2-3, the sermon encouraged Carey's fellow Baptists to trust God and venture forth to the nations with the message of the gospel with the confidence that God would bless that message and extend his kingdom. We do not know the details of the sermon that Carey preached, since no copy of it exists. What we do know are the two main divisions of his message: 'Let us expect great things. Let us attempt great things.'

Finally, Carey wrote a book that was published in 1792 and is entitled *An Enquiry into the Obligations of Christians, to Use Means for the Conversion of the Heathens*. This work is divided into five sections, which:

1. Discuss the theological implications of Matthew 28:19-20;
2. Outline the history of missions since the days of the apostles;
3. Survey the state of the world in Carey's day, especially with regard to religion and population;
4. Answer various objections to sending out missionaries;
5. Indicate immediate practical steps that could be taken.

The treatise has been well described as the greatest missionary treatise in the English language. Overall, this book reveals Carey's successful marriage of a deep-seated conviction in God's sovereignty in salvation with an equally profound belief that in converting sinners God uses means.[29] The influence of Andrew Fuller and his thought is here abundantly plain.

A wretched, poor and helpless worm'

Two passages from the final section of the treatise well reveal Carey's convictions immediately prior to his going out to India in 1793.

One of the first, and most important of those duties which are incumbent upon us, is fervent and united prayer. However the influence of the Holy Spirit may be set at nought, and run down by many, it will be found upon trial, that all means which we can use, without it, will be ineffectual. If a temple is raised for God in the heathen world, it will not be by might, nor by power, nor by the authority of the magistrate, or the eloquence of the orator; but by my Spirit, saith the Lord of Hosts.[30] *We must therefore be in real earnest in supplicating his blessing upon our labours.*

It is represented in the prophets, that when there shall be a great mourning in the land, as the mourning of Hadadrimmon in the valley of Megiddon, and every family shall mourn apart, and their wives apart, it shall all follow upon a spirit of grace, and supplication. And when these things shall take place, it is promised that there shall be a fountain opened for the house of David, and for the inhabitants of Jerusalem, for sin, and for uncleanness, — and that the idols shall be destroyed, and the false prophets ashamed of their profession. Zech 12:10,14 - 13:1,6. This prophecy seems to teach that when there shall be an universal conjunction in fervent prayer, and all shall esteem Zion's welfare as their own, then copious influences of the Spirit shall be shed upon the churches, which like a purifying fountain shall cleanse the servants of the Lord. Nor shall this cleansing influence stop here; all old idolatrous prejudices shall be rooted out, and truth prevail so gloriously that false teachers shall be so ashamed as rather to wish to be classed with obscure herdsmen, or the meanest peasants, than bear the ignominy attendant on their detection.

The most glorious works of grace that have ever took place, have been in answer to prayer; and it is in this way, we have the greatest reason to suppose, that the glorious out-pouring of the Spirit, which we expect at last, will be bestowed. With respect to our own immediate connections, we have within these few years been favoured with some tokens for good, granted in answer to prayer, which should encourage us to persist, and increase in that important duty. I trust our monthly prayer-meetings for the success of the gospel have not been in vain.[31]

Carey is writing against the background of the movement of regular prayer-meetings for revival which had been going on in Baptist circles since 1784 and that has been noted above in chapter 4.[32]

Prayer is indispensable — but prayer must be linked to action, as Carey went on to emphasize:

Suppose a company of serious Christians, ministers and private persons, were to form themselves into a society, and make a number of rules respecting the regulation of the plan, and the persons who are to be employed as missionaries, the means of defraying the expense, etc. This society must consist of persons whose hearts are in the work, men of serious religion, and possessing a spirit of perseverance; there must be a determination not to admit any person who is not of this description, or to retain him longer than he answers to it.[33]

Here Carey was drawing upon a tradition in English Protestant circles in which voluntary, religious associations were formed in order to achieve specific goals. What Carey formulated here in print was realized at Kettering later that year. On 2 October 1792 fourteen men, including Carey, Fuller, Ryland and Sutcliff met in the back parlour of the home of a Martha Wallis (d. 1812), the widow of a deacon of Kettering Baptist Church, and formed 'The Particular Baptist Society for propagating the Gospel amongst the

Heathen' (later simply known as The Baptist Missionary Society). William Carey, aged thirty-one years, became the society's first appointee, along with John Thomas (1757–1801), a surgeon who had already spent time in India.[34]

The Serampore Mission

Carey, his family, and Thomas arrived in Calcutta in November 1793, but within a short space of time Carey and his family ran out of money and he was compelled to take work as the manager of a new indigo factory at a village called Mudnabatti, around 280 miles north of Calcutta. Life here was far from easy, for the place was remote and unhealthy. One of Carey's sons, Peter, died, aged only five. His wife Dorothy, who had been deeply reluctant to go to India in the first place, had a total mental breakdown and was soon in a state of helpless insanity.[35] Carey spent five years in this remote village. Three things came out of this time of great trial. First, Carey acquired an extensive knowledge of the Bengali language. Second, as soon as he had mastered elements of Bengali, he began work on the translation of the New Testament. Third, his trials with Dorothy's mental state and other challenges forced him to develop a deeper trust in God.

In late 1799 Carey moved to Serampore, a Danish colony fourteen miles north of Calcutta on the west bank of the River Hooghly and linked up with two new missionaries who had just arrived from England. William Ward was a printer whom Carey had met in England and who would become the best preacher at Serampore. During his younger years he had been involved in radical politics — a leaning and inclination he put forever behind him when he went out to India. The other missionary was Joshua Marshman, an extremely industrious individual who was imbued with deep learning, but one whose mind sometimes worked 'without any clear order or coherence'. He became the foreign secretary of the mission.

So began the Serampore Mission, based around the partnership of these three men, a partnership which has few parallels in Christian history, and a work which, in the words of William Wilberforce (1759–1833), became 'one of the chief glories of our country'.[36] In all of the extant literature and manuscripts of these three men there is amazingly no trace of mutual jealousy or severe anger. Henry Martyn (1781–1812), an Evangelical Anglican and missionary to the Persians, said that never were 'such men … so suited to another and to their work'.[37]

Krishna Pal

Within a year of beginning the mission at Serampore, converts began to come in. The first was Krishna Pal (1764–1822), a thirty-six-year-old carpenter. Pal had heard the gospel through Moravian missionaries some time before, but it had had little impact. On 26 November 1800, though, he fell and dislocated his shoulder. Having heard that there was a doctor at Serampore, the Indian carpenter sought out John Thomas. He helped set Krishna Pal's dislocated arm and also took the opportunity to share the gospel with Pal.

The Indian returned a few days later to tell Thomas and the other Baptist missionaries that he knew himself to be 'a very great sinner'. But he had confessed his sins and had 'obtained', he told them, the 'righteousness of Jesus Christ; and I am free'.[38] Pal declared himself ready to break caste, something that was rightly required by the Serampore missionaries, and be baptized. He was subsequently baptized by Carey on Sunday 28 December 1800, in the Hooghly River. William Ward, Carey's missionary co-worker, wrote thus in his diary of this baptism: 'Thus the door of faith is open to the gentiles; who shall shut it? The chain of the caste is broken; who shall mend it?'[39] By 1812 there were 300 converts,[40] and by 1838, four years after Carey's death in 1834, some 2,500–3,000 had come to embrace Christ as their Saviour either through the mission at Serampore or one of its preaching stations.

'The Wyclif of the East'[41]

By the time that Carey moved to Serampore he had acquired a remarkably extensive knowledge of Bengali.[42] Moreover, as soon as he had mastered the elements of the Bengali language he had begun work on the translation of the New Testament. This Bengali New Testament would eventually progress through eight editions, each of them incorporating revisions, and sometimes involving a complete re-translation. In time Carey would go on to do translations in five of the great languages of India: Bengali, Sanskrit, Marathi, Hindi and Oriya. Although Sanskrit was no longer a spoken language at the time when Carey was in India, Carey soon realized that Indians regarded this language as the only language worthy of literary production. It was a classical language that functioned much like Latin did in Europe during the Middle Ages. Carey realized that if the Bible were to be taken seriously by Indian religious leaders, it had to be translated into Sanskrit. Sanskrit was also the basis for many other Indian languages, so Carey hoped that a translation into this language would make the task of translating the Scriptures into other languages easier. In total, Carey translated or supervised the translation of the Scriptures into thirty-four languages or dialects. In fact, in these early years of the modern missionary movement, forty-three per cent of first translations of the Scriptures into new languages anywhere in the world were published at Serampore.

As a grammarian Carey was brilliant. As a translator, though, it must be admitted that he lacked 'a keen sensitiveness to the finer shades and nuances of ideas and meaning', a failing which dogged all of his translations.[43] Carey remarked frequently that he knew the translations were not perfect and he hoped that others would build on them. Carey believed that a translation should be geared as much as possible to the grammatical structure and wording of the original Hebrew or Greek. But in doing so he failed to make the Scriptures communicate in the living language of the people of India. It is not fortuitous that the translation which survived the longest was his translation into Sanskrit. It was thirty-three years before it was replaced with a new translation. Perhaps it lasted longer because it was a classical, written language, and not a spoken, vernacular language. Carey's failure to understand at times the subtleties of translation was, it should be noted, a common failing of the day among translators. A good exception is Adoniram Judson's translation of the Scriptures into Burmese. His Burmese Bible is still in use, and has remained readable, whereas none of Carey's translations are still in use.

Driving Carey, though, was the conviction that the Word of God had to be available to the people-groups that he was trying to reach, for it is the Word that converts and matures Christians.[44] Yet, Carey would have probably achieved more if he had attempted less.

'Endless glory'

Carey laboured in India until his death in 1834. The impact of his missionary labours can be well seen in the following extract from a letter by the Anglican evangelical Thomas Scott (1747–1821), who had known Carey in his early years. Writing on 3 December 1814, to John Ryland Jr, Scott stated:

> *I do most heartily rejoice in what your missionaries are doing in India. Their's is the most regular and best conducted plan against the kingdom of darkness that modern times have shewn; and I augur the most extensive success. More genuine*

Christian wisdom, fortitude, and disinterested assiduity, perseverance, and patience appear, than I elsewhere read of. May God protect and prosper! May all India be peopled with true Christians!   even though they be all baptists … The Lord is doing great things, and answering prayer everywhere.[45]

'The Lord is doing great things': Carey had ventured out to India because of his great expectation that God would do 'great things' for his own glory and for his kingdom. And so it had proven. But as Carey drew towards the end of his life, his thoughts were focused as much on God's supreme work in the crucified Christ as on his exploits in India. Thus, he informed his sisters in 1831: 'The atoning sacrifice made by our Lord on the cross is the ground of my hope of acceptance, pardon, justification, sanctification, and endless glory.'[46]

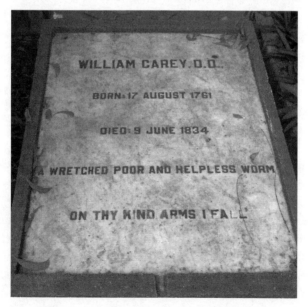

The tomb of William Carey at Serampore
(picture courtesy of Keith Edwards)

A concluding word

An excellent summation of the significance of the revival that came to the English Baptists at the close of the long eighteenth century can be seen in the following quote from the pen of Thomas Chalmers (1780–1847), who was probably the leading Scottish Presbyterian divine of his day as well as being a friend of Andrew Fuller.

Let it never be forgotten of the Particular Baptists of England that they form the denomination of [Andrew] Fuller and [William] Carey and [John] Ryland [Jr.] and [Robert Hall [Jr.] and [John] Foster; that they have originated among the greatest of all missionary enterprises; that they have enriched the Christian literature of our country with authorship of the most exalted piety as well as of the first talent and the first eloquence; that they have waged a very noble and successful war with the hydra of Antinomianism; that perhaps there is not a more intellectual community of ministers in our island or who have put forth to their number a greater amount of mental power and mental activity in the defence and illustration of our common faith; and, what is better than all the triumph of genius or understanding, who, by their zeal and fidelity and pastoral labour among the congregations which they have reared, have done more to swell the lists of genuine discipleship in the walks of private society — and thus both to uphold and to extend the living Christianity of our nation.[1]

Here Chalmers took note of four ways in which the Calvinistic Baptist community in England had been a blessing to the larger Church in the British Isles — and he would not have erred if he had referred that blessing to the Church further afield.

First, there was the area of missions. It was among this community that the Baptist Missionary Society had been formed in 1792, William Carey sent out to the Indian subcontinent, and others to that field and other places of missionary service. And it was especially Carey, more than any other figure, who was the exemplar of missions for the world of nineteenth-century Evangelicalism. Second, Chalmers drew attention to various books from Baptist authors that were marked by both piety and literary excellence and that had blessed the people of God. Then, there was the way that Baptists had been used in the defence of the Christian faith against various theological errors, one of which he mentions specifically, namely Antinomianism. Chalmers may well have been especially thinking of Andrew Fuller, whom he had mentioned by name earlier in the text,[2] but there were other fine Baptist apologists whom he could have had in mind. Finally, 'better than all the triumph of genius or understanding', Chalmers is thankful for the faithful labours of Calvinistic Baptist pastors, which have produced so many godly followers of Christ. In fine, in this quote, we see at a glance the fruits of true revival: mission, enriching Christian literature, ardent love for the truth, and the making of disciples of Christ in all walks of life.

Not long before Samuel Pearce died, Andrew Fuller informed him that he had plans to write a memoir of Pearce's life. 'You need not fear,' he wrote to Pearce on 30 August 1799, however, 'that I will puff off³ your character any more than you would mine. We are all of us, God knows it, poor unworthy creatures. Yet the truth may be told to the glory of sovereign grace...'⁴ Similarly, the telling of the story of revival in this book, though rooted in a sincere love for these Baptists, has been written not to puff them up, but for 'the glory of sovereign grace' of the Triune God.

Appendix:

Eighteenth-century Baptists
and the gifts of the Holy Spirit in revival[1]

It has been frequently the case in twentieth- and early twenty-first century thinking about revival to associate it with a re-occurrence of what are called the 'extraordinary' gifts of the Holy Spirit, namely, such things as prophecy, words of knoweldge, visions, healings, and speaking in tongues. But this is not the way revival has traditionally been conceived, as this appendix will argue from the case of the late eighteenth-century Baptist experience.

The revival that came to the Calvinistic Baptist denomination between the 1780s and the 1820s, which we have looked at in this book, did so with remarkably few of the unusual manifestations that occurred in the early years of the First Great Awakening from the 1730s to the 1750s, things like visions and collapsing physically under the sound of the gospel. Moreover, in continuity with most other eighteenth-century evangelicals,[2] the Calvinistic Baptists of this period of revival did not seek the so-called extraordinary gifts of the Spirit. For example, in a sermon that John Ryland Jr preached on 1 Corinthians 14:8 in 1813, he unequivocally declared regarding the abuse of glossolalia in the first-century church of Corinth that 'no one is *now* in danger of falling into precisely the same mistake, because the gift of tongues has long ceased'.[3] Ryland believed that the extraordinary gifts of the Spirit were given to the Church in the apostolic age in order to validate the initial preaching of the gospel. Such gifts were bestowed 'for the purpose of attesting the truth, at its first publication'.[4] Ryland seems to have regularly drawn a contrast between the extraordinary gifts of the Spirit and his 'ordinary influences'. As he stated in a sermon entitled 'The Love of the Spirit', which was based on Romans 15:30:

> *The ordinary influences of the Holy Spirit are of far more importance to the individuals who partake of them, than his extraordinary gifts; that is, it is better to be a saint than a prophet; better to be made holy, than to be inspired; better to be directed into the love of God, than into the knowledge of futurity. Herein the blessed Spirit communicates himself in his own proper nature, as the Spirit of holiness.*[5,6]

Why did Ryland believe that the 'ordinary influences of the Holy Spirit' are of greater import than 'his extraordinary gifts'? The former impart personal holiness, and it is only those who have experience of these 'sanctifying influences' of the Spirit who can have any legitimate assurance of eternal life. Those who are indwelt by the sanctifying Spirit are 'sealed to the day of redemption' and stamped for an eternity in heaven. The 'extraordinary gifts' of the Spirit, on the other hand, give no such assurance, for there is no inseparable connection between the gifts and holiness. In other words, the presence of the fruit of the Spirit is evidence of salvation, whereas that of his gifts is not.

As for the unusual manifestations witnessed during the early years of the First Great Awakening, Baptists like Ryland were quite willing to acknowledge their genuineness. However, they were not at all convinced that they were necessary for the advance of God's kingdom. Ryland's close friend, William Carey, wrote a marvellous letter to his sister Mary in 1789 that discussed these manifestations. Evidently she was wrestling with assurance of salvation, and so he asked her:

> *Do you doubt because you have not seen visions, heard voices, or felt impulses? This I know is what many Christians place dependence upon. But suppose that you have felt nothing of all this, there is no reason for you to despair; and if you have been favoured with repeated instances of this nature this is no proof of your Christianity. I apprehend that too many place too much confidence in things of this nature and make a shining light, an audible voice, or the sudden application of a passage of Scripture an evidence of their being the children of God. But where is the part of God's Word that informs us of any such evidence of religion as these are? Or if a person had no other evidence than such, would you, could you encourage him to depend or take comfort from this? That these are extraordinary interpositions of Divine Power upon extraordinary occasions I don't deny but 'tis God and not us that must judge of the emergency of our case; and even if he does interpose in a singular way, 'tis the matter and not the manner of his interposition that we ought to depend upon, and that not as an evidence of grace but as a Divine support in the path of duty. No doubt but the tempter is aware of the taste of the age and therefore endeavours to seduce us by things miraculous to which the mind of man is much prone, and while we thus listen to his devices and limit the Holy One of Israel we distress ourselves and dishonour him. But we have a more sure word of Prophecy whereunto we do well that we take heed.*[7]

Carey did not deny that such unusual phenomena as 'a shining light' or 'an audible voice' could be from God. But such occurrences were given according to God's sovereignty, and not according to man's desire. Moreover, these experiences were no proof that the subject of them genuinely knew God. 'Real religion', Carey went on to emphasize in the letter, consisted of things quite different: 'repentance, faith, obedience, submission, zeal and consolation'.

Yet, it needs noting that late eighteenth-century Calvinistic Baptists like Ryland and Carey had a great hunger and desire for the Spirit's presence and power, as the following text bears witness. It was written by Ryland in 1792, at the height of the French Revolution, as part of a circular letter sent out by the Northamptonshire Association to its member churches.

> *Surely the state both of the world, and of church, calls loudly upon us all to persist in wrestling instantly with God, for greater effusions of his Holy Spirit ... Let us not cease crying mightily unto the Lord, 'until the Spirit be poured upon us from on high' [Isaiah 32:15]; then the wilderness shall become as a fruitful field, and the desert like the garden of God. Yes, beloved, the Scriptures cannot be broken. Jesus must reign universally. All nations shall own him. All people shall serve him. His kingdom shall be extended, not by human might, or power, but by the effusion of His Holy Spirit [cf. Zechariah 4:6].*[8]

This text is redolent with the pneumatological thought of Jonathan Edwards, who, as we have seen, was mentor to both Ryland and Carey. There is the emphasis on patient but diligent prayer for the outpouring of the Holy Spirit, and the optimism regarding the irresistible advance of Jesus' kingdom throughout the world by the power of the outpoured Spirit. Such are the signs and wonders which Ryland and Carey, genuine heirs of Edwards, longed to see.

Notes

Introduction

1. Michael R. Watts, *The Dissenters* (Oxford: Clarendon Press, 1978), 222.
2. William is often portrayed by historians as a committed Calvinist. However, in a recent study of William's religious commitment, Jonathan I. Israel has argued that William's personal religiosity was 'decidedly tepid', despite the fact that as a young boy he had been under the tutelage of Cornelius Trigland, a pillar of Dutch Calvinism ['William III and Toleration' in Ole Peter Grell, Jonathan I. Israel, and Nicholas Tyacke, eds, *From Persecution to Toleration. The Glorious Revolution and Religion in England* (Oxford: Clarendon Press, 1991), 129–170].
3. *The Evangelical Revival* (London/New York: Routledge, 1998), 35.
4. Letter to Stephen West, 17 September 1816 ['Contributions to History', *The Bibliotheca Sacra and Theological Eclectic*, 30 (1873), 186–7].
5. Cited David Kingdon, 'C. H. Spurgeon and the Down Grade Controversy' in *The Good Fight of Faith* (London: The Westminster Conference/The Evangelical Press, 1971), 48.
6. For a somewhat different reading of the events covered in this book and therefore of this revival, see Andrew Christopher Smith, '"Joy cometh in the morning": An Examination of the Gradual Nature of the Moderation of 18th-century Particular Baptist Theology' (Unpublished paper, summer 2001).

Chapter 1

1. Cited W. E. Blomfield, 'Yorkshire Baptist Churches in the 17th and 18th Centuries' in *The Baptists of Yorkshire* (2nd ed.; Bradford and London: Wm Byles & Sons Ltd/London: Kingsgate Press, 1912), 105.
2. For the story of these churches in the seventeenth century, see Michael A. G. Haykin, *Kiffin, Knollys and Keach: Rediscovering Our English Baptist Heritage* (Leeds: Reformation Today Trust, 1996).

3. Cited Joseph Ivimey, *A History of the English Baptists* (London: B. J. Holdsworth, 1823), III, 277.

4. *The Christian Life, In Divers of its Branches, Described and Recommended* (London: Aaron Ward, 1746) II, ix. See also his *A Humble Address to the Churches of Christ* (London: J. Ward, 1750), 1; *The Christian Salutation* (London, 1766), iv; *The Scripture-Doctrine of Christ's Sonship* (London, 1771), v–vi. On the growth of Wallin's own congregation at Maze Pond, see R. Philip Roberts, *Continuity and Change. London Calvinistic Baptists and The Evangelical Revival 1760-1820* (Wheaton, Illinois: Richard Owen Roberts, Publishers, 1989), 71.

5. *Exhortations, Relating to Prayer and the Lord's Supper* (London: John Ward, 1752), viii, x. See also his *Humble Address*, 16, 18; *The Redeemer's Charge Against his Declining Churches, Exemplified in the Case of the Church of Ephesus; And applied to the State of Religion in the Present Time* (London: J. Ward, 1748), 25.

6. 'The Baptist Interest under George I', *Transactions of the Baptist Historical Society*, 2 (1910–1911), 95–109.

7. 'Baptist Interest under George I', 108. See also the meticulous analysis of the Evans list and other relevant sources by Michael R. Watts, *The Dissenters* (Oxford: Clarendon Press, 1978), 267–71, 491–510, who concurs with Whitley's estimate.

8. 'Baptist Ministers in England about 1750 A.D', *Transactions of the Baptist Historical Society*, 6 (1918–1919), 138–57. See also Alan D. Gilbert, *Religion and Society in Industrial England. Church, Chapel and Social Change, 1740-1914* (London/New York: Longman Group Ltd., 1976), 35, 37.

9. See also C. E. Fryer, 'The Numerical Decline of Dissent in England Previous to the Industrial Revolution', *The American Journal of Theology*, 17 (1913), 232–39; Deryck W. Lovegrove, *Established Church, Sectarian People. Itinerary and the transformation of English Dissent, 1780-1830* (Cambridge: Cambridge University Press, 1988), 38.

10. 'Discipline of the English and Scottish Baptist Churches' in *The Complete Works of the Rev. Andrew Fuller*, revised Joseph Belcher (1845 ed.; repr. Harrisonburg, Virginia: Sprinkle Publications, 1988), III, 478.

11. I am deeply thankful to Pastor Ken Hart, of Cradley Chapel, Cradley, Worcestershire, who reminded me of this at the 2010 Revival Conference of the Wales Evangelical School of Theology.

12. Paul Langford, *A Polite and Commercial People: England 1727-1783* (Oxford: Clarendon Press, 1989), 257.

13. W. T. Whitley, *A History of British Baptists* (2nd ed.; London: The Kingsgate Press, 1932), 215–6.

14. 'Reverend Henry Phillips (1719-1789): His Testimony', *Irish Baptist Historical Society Journal*, 17 (1984–1985), 34.

15. Dora Yates, *The Baptists in Colne* (Colne: n.p., 1985), 12–13. It is interesting to note that Baptists in the era under discussion often defended the practice of believer's baptism in such inclement weather with accounts of how even the sick who were so baptized suffered no ill effects, and sometimes, were even

healed in the act of being baptized. See, for example, Stephen A. Swaine, 'The Gifford Remains. No. II', *The Baptist Magazine*, 79 (1887), 213–4.

16. Thomas Steadman, *Memoir of the Rev. William Steadman, D.D.* (London, 1838), 234–5. For this quote, I am indebted to Sharon James, 'Revival and Renewal in Baptist Life: The Contribution of William Steadman (1764–1837)', *The Baptist Quarterly*, 37 (1997–1998), 268–9.

17. Cited G. M. Ditchfield, *The Evangelical Revival* (London/New York: Routledge, 1998), 54–5. I am deeply grateful to Mr Nigel Pibworth of Biggleswade, Bedfordshire, England, for first drawing my attention to this excellent overview of the revivals of the eighteenth century.

18. Cited John Ryland, *The Work of Faith, the Labour of Love, and the Patience of Hope, illustrated; in the Life and Death of the Rev. Andrew Fuller* (2nd ed.; London: Button & Son, 1818), 12.

19. *The Gospel Worthy of All Acceptation* (*Complete Works of the Rev. Andrew Fuller*, II, 329).

20. Ditchfield, *Evangelical Revival*, 39.

21. Cited Eifion Evans, *Daniel Rowland and the Great Evangelical Awakening in Wales* (Edinburgh: The Banner of Truth Trust, 1985), 243.

22. *Jonathan Edwards: Letters and Personal Writings*, ed. George S. Claghorn (*The Works of Jonathan Edwards*, vol. 16; New Haven/London: Yale University Press, 1998), 79.

23. Cited John R. Tyson, ed., *Charles Wesley. A Reader* (New York/Oxford: Oxford University Press, 1989), 418.

24. Ivimey, *History of the English Baptists*, III, 280.

25. *Light broke forth in Wales, expelling darkness* (London, 1696), 250.

26. *Gospel Mysteries Unveiled: or, An Exposition of All the Parables and Many Similitudes spoken by Our Lord and Savior Jesus Christ* (London: L. I. Higham, 1815), II, 383.

27. Cited Dafydd Densil James Morgan, 'The Development of the Baptist Movement in Wales between 1714 and 1815 with particular reference to the Evangelical Revival' (Unpublished D. Phil. Thesis, Regent's Park College, University of Oxford, 1986), 39–40.

28. *The Dissenters' Reasons For separating from the Church of England* (London: G. Keith, 1751), 102, 104. The first edition of this pamphlet was attached to Gill's *The Argument from Apostolic Tradition, In Favour of Infant-Baptism* (London: G. Keith, 1751). *Dissenters' Reasons* can be found on pages 100–19. Gill's pamphlet proved to be fairly popular, going through four editions in less than ten years.

29. *Dissenters' Reasons*, 104.

30. *Dissenters' Reasons*, 105–14.

31. *Dissenters' Reasons*, 116–7.

32. *Dissenters' Reasons*, 118.

33. *Dissenters' Reasons*, 119.

34. Cited Charles B. Jewson, 'St. Mary's, Norwich', *The Baptist Quarterly*, 10 (1940–1941), 283.

35. R. Philip Roberts, *Continuity and Change. London Calvinistic Baptists and*

The Evangelical Revival 1760–1820 (Wheaton: Illinois: Richard Owen Roberts Publishers, 1989), 81.

36. Cited James M. Renihan, 'The Puritan Roots of Reformed Baptists' (Unpublished paper, 12 March 1998), 24.

37. *The Living Water: or, the Work of the Spirit as the Sanctifier and Comforter of Believers in Jesus* (London, 1746), 17–18.

38. William C. Placher, *The Domestication of Transcendence. How Modern Thinking about God Went Wrong* (Louisville, Kentucky: Westminster John Knox Press, 1996), 164–78; Philip Dixon, *'Nice and Hot Disputes': The Doctrine of the Trinity in the Seventeenth Century* (London/New York: T & T Clark, 2003). The quote is from Dixon, *Nice and Hot Disputes',* 212.

39. G. L. Bray, 'Trinity' in *New Dictionary of Theology,* eds Sinclair B. Ferguson, David F. Wright, and J. I. Packer (Downers Grove, Illinois/Leicester: InterVarsity Press, 1988), 694.

40. *The Doctrine of the Trinity, Stated and Vindicated* (London: Aaron Ward, 1731), 203–4. For a good example of the serious light in which Gill viewed deviation from the doctrine of the Trinity, see Sayer Rudd, *Impartial Reflections on the Minute Which The Author received, from The Ministers of The Calvinistical Baptist Board, by the hands of Mess. Gill and Brine* (London, 1736).

41. *A Complete Body of Doctrinal and Practical Divinity* 1.31.

42. *A Brief Memoir of the Life and Writings of the late Rev. John Gill, D.D.* (Repr. Harrisonburg, Virginia: Gano Books, 1992), 127–8.

Chapter 2

1. The section of this chapter on Benjamin Francis has already appeared as Michael A. G. Haykin, 'Benjamin Francis (1734–1799)' in his ed., *British Particular Baptists, 1638–1910* (Springfield, Missouri: Particular Baptist Press, 2000), II, 16–29. Used by permission.

2. See the detailed argument in this regard by Roger Hayden, *Continuity and Change: Evangelical Calvinism among eighteenth-century Baptist ministers trained at Bristol Academy, 1690–1791* (Milton under Wychwood, Chipping Norton, Oxfordshire: Nigel Lynn Publishing, 2006).

3. Helpful in writing this paragraph and the next has been James M. Renihan, 'A Tale of Two Associations' (Unpublished paper, March, 1997).

4. *The English Baptists of the Eighteenth Century* (London: The Baptist Historical Society, 1986), 84–5.

5. For the life of Francis, the following sources have been extremely helpful: Thomas Flint, 'A Brief Narrative of the Life and Death of the Rev. Benjamin Francis, A.M.', annexed to John Ryland Jr, *The Presence of Christ the Source of eternal Bliss. A Funeral Discourse,…occasioned by the Death of the Rev. Benjamin Francis, A.M.* (Bristol, 1800), 33–76; Geoffrey F. Nuttall, 'Questions and Answers: An Eighteenth-Century Correspondence', *The Baptist Quarterly,* 27 (1977–1978), 83–90; *idem,* 'Letters by Benjamin Francis', *Trafodion* (1983), 4–8. I have also benefited from Gwyn Davies, 'A Welsh Exile: Benjamin Francis (1734–99)' (Unpublished ms., 1999), 3 pages. There is a portrait of Francis in John Rippon, ed., *The Baptist Annual Register,* 2 (1794–1797), opposite page 327.

Notes

6. Nuttall, 'Letters by Benjamin Francis', 7; The Minute Book of Carter Lane Church, 1719–July 1808 (The Deacons Vestry, the Metropolitan Tabernacle, London): Entries for 10 February, 13 April, and 22 June 1772. I am grateful to Dr Peter Masters, Pastor of the Metropolitan Tabernacle, for permission to consult this minute book. On the significance of Gill's mention of Francis as a possible successor, see Raymond Brown, *The English Baptists of the 18th Century* (London: The Baptist Historical Society, 1986), 94.

7. Letter to Caleb Evans, 22 February 1772 (cited Nuttall, 'Letters by Benjamin Francis', 7–8).

8. Dafydd Densil James Morgan, 'The Development of the Baptist Movement in Wales between 1714 and 1815 with particular reference to the Evangelical Revival' (Unpublished D. Phil. Thesis, Regent's Park College, University of Oxford, 1986), 59. For further information on Enoch Francis, see Flint, 'Brief Narrative', 33–7; Morgan, 'Development of the Baptist Movement in Wales', *passim*.

9. For a brief account of the early history of the Horsley church, see Albion M. Urdank, *Religion and Society in a Cotswold Vale. Nailsworth, Gloucestershire, 1780–1865* (Berkeley: University of California Press, 1990), 90–3.

10. Cited Urdank, *Religion and Society*, 95; Nuttall, 'Letters by Benjamin Francis', 6. In one of the circular letters that he drew up for the Western Association, he mentions that some of his readers are 'sorely distressed with pressing indigence' [*Circular Letter of the Western Association* (1772), 3].

11. Davies, 'Welsh Exile', 2. On Francis' financial problems, see also Flint, 'Brief Narrative', 49.

12. Flint, 'Brief Narrative', 49–52.

13. Benjamin Francis, 'Obituary: Miss Hester Francis' in John Rippon, ed., *The Baptist Annual Register*, 1 (1790–1793), 158–9.

14. *Circular Letter of the Western Association* (1800), 2.

15. 'A List of the Particular Baptist Churches in England, 1798' in John Rippon, ed., *The Baptist Annual Register*, 3 (1798–1801), 14–15.

16. 'Brief Narrative', 45–6. The names of the towns and villages referred to by Flint have been modernized according to current spelling. On Francis' itinerant ministry, see further Brown, *English Baptists of the 18th Century*, 115, 122–3, 124.

17. See the informative discussion of travel in this period and the following century by Sven Birkerts, *The Gutenberg Elegies: The Fate of Reading in an Electronic Age* (New York: Fawcett Columbine, 1994), 24–5.

18. See, for example, *The Conflagaration* (Bristol, 1770) or *The Association* (in Rippon, ed., *Baptist Annual Register*, 2:17–20).

19. For instance, *The Socinian Champion or priestleyan divinity* (London: T. Bensley, 1788) is a critique of the Unitarianism of Joseph Priestley (1733–1804), while *The Oracle* (1799) takes issue with the General, i.e. Arminian, Baptists.

20. See *An Elegy on the Death of the Rev. John Gill* (London, 1772); *Elegy on George Whitefield* (Bristol, 1771); *An Elegy on Mr. Pearce* (annexed to Ryland, *Presence of Christ*). For Pearce, see below, Chapter 6.

21. 'Brief Narrative', 47.

22. A remark about his preaching that appeared after his death in the *Circular Letter of the Western Association* (1800), 2.
23. 'The Association' in Rippon, ed., *Baptist Annual Register*, 1:17, 18, 20.
24. *The Beauty of Social Religion; or, The Nature and Glory of a Gospel Church* (Circular Letter of the Northamptonshire Association, 1777), 2.
25. For the early history of this association, see Geoffrey F. Nuttall, 'The Baptist Western Association 1653–1658', *The Journal of Ecclesiastical History*, 15 (1964), 213–8. For a somewhat inadequate history of the association up to the mid-nineteenth century, see J. G. Fuller, *A Brief History of the Western Association* (Bristol, 1843).
26. *Circular Letter of the Western Association* (1772), 3–4.
27. *Circular Letter of the Western Association* (1772), 4.
28. *Circular Letter of the Western Association* (1772), 5.
29. *Circular Letter of the Western Association* (1772), 5.
30. *Circular Letter of the Western Association* (1772), 5.
31. *Circular Letter of the Western Association* (1778), 3.
32. Cited Flint, 'Brief Narrative', 56–7.
33. Cited Flint, 'Brief Narrative', 58–9.
34. For material on Anne Steele, see Karen Smith, 'The Community and the Believers: A Study of Calvinistic Baptist Spirituality in Some Towns and Villages of Hampshire and the Borders of Wiltshire, c.1730-1830' (Unpublished DPhil. dissertation, University of Oxford, 1986); J. R. Broome, *A Bruised Reed: The Life and Times of Anne Steele* (Harpenden, Hertfordshire: Gospel Standard Trust Publications, 2007); Nancy Jiwon Cho, '"The Ministry of Song": Unmarried British Women's Hymn Writing, 1760–1936' (Unpublished Ph.D. thesis, Durham University, 2007), 43–84; Cynthia Y. Aalders, *To Express the Ineffable: The Hymns and Spirituality of Anne Steele* (Milton Keynes/Colorado Springs/Hyderabad: Paternoster, 2008); and Priscilla Chan, 'Anne Steele's Spiritual Vision: Seeing God in the Peaks, Valleys and Plateaus of Life' (Unpublished MTS thesis, Toronto Baptist Seminary, 2010).
35. Some of her suffering, though, especially the story of a fiancé being drowned on their wedding day, appears to be apocryphal. See Jiwon Cho, 'The Ministry of Song', 43–8. I am indebted to Matthew Crawford, currently doing doctoral studies at Durham University, for access to this thesis.
36. Anne Steele Papers, STE 3/10 iii (Angus Library, Regent's Park College, Oxford).
37. Jiwon Cho, 'The Ministry of Song', 77–8.
38. *A Collection of Hymns Adapted to Public Worship* (3rd ed.; Bristol: W. Pine, 1778), Hymn 145.
39. On the free offer of the gospel in Steele's hymns, see further Sharon James, *In Trouble and in Joy: Four Women who Lived for God* (Darlington, England: Evangelical Press, 2003), 154.

Chapter 3

1. *To Change the World: The Irony, Tragedy, and Possibility of Christianity in the Late Modern World* (Oxford University Press, 2010), 38.

Notes

2. *To Change the World*, 38.
3. Letter, 7 September 1822 in Hugh Anderson, *The Life and Letters of Christopher Anderson* (Edinburgh: W. P. Kennedy, 1854), 379.
4. David Phillips, *Memoir of the Life, Labors, and Extensive Usefulness of the Rev. Christmas Evans* (New York: M W. Dodd, 1843), 74.
5. John Ryland Jr, *The Indwelling and Righteousness of Christ No Security against Corporal Death, but the Source of Spiritual and Eternal Life* (London: W. Button & Son, 1815), 35–6. These words are actually used by Ryland of his friendship with Fuller, but they can also be applied to the friendship between Sutcliff, Fuller and Ryland. In the 'Postscript' to this sermon, Ryland describes Sutcliff and Fuller as 'my dearest brethren' (*Indwelling and Righteousness of Christ*, 47). In his *The Work of Faith, the Labour of Love, and the Patience of Hope, illustrated; in the Life and Death of the Rev. Andrew Fuller* (2nd ed.; London: Button & Son, 1818), ix, Ryland states that he always regarded Fuller and 'Brother Sutcliff, and myself, as more closely united to each other, than either of us were to anyone else'.
6. Diogenes Allen, *Love: Christian Romance, Marriage, Friendship* (Cambridge, Massachusetts: Cowley Publications, 1987), 45–6.
7. 'Staving Off Despair: On the Use and Abuse of Pessimism for Life', *Standpoint* (September 2010), 36, col.1.
8. *The Screwtape Letters*, Letter 10 in *The Best of C. S. Lewis* (Washington, D.C.: Canon Press, 1969), 43.
9. 'Friendship', *Dictionary of Biblical Imagery*, eds Leland Ryken *et al.* (Downers Grove, Illinois/Leicester: InterVarsity Press, 1998), 308–9.
10. On John Collett Ryland, see Peter Naylor, 'John Collett Ryland (1723–1792)' in Michael A. G. Haykin, ed., *British Particular Baptists, 1638–1910* (Springfield, Missouri: Particular Baptist Press, 1998), I, 184–201.
11. In John Rippon, ed., *The Baptist Annual Register*, 3 (London, 1801), 366.
12. This interweaving of piety and theological reflection is well seen in a phrase that Ryland inserted in a printed copy of an ordination sermon by Samuel Spring (1746–1819), a New England preacher who was married to the daughter of the New Divinity theologian Samuel Hopkins (1721–1803). At the point where Spring is describing the depth of the well of theology and that 'fresh and pure water' can only be drawn out of this well by 'hard study', Ryland has added 'prayer &' just before 'hard study' [Geoffrey F. Nuttall, 'Some of John Ryland's Books', *The Baptist Quarterly*, 33 (1989–1990), 214].
13. The earliest memoir of Ryland is that found at the conclusion of the sermon Robert Hall Jr preached at Ryland's funeral: 'A Sermon Occasioned by the death of the Rev. John Ryland, D.D., preached at the Baptist Meeting, Broadmead, Bristol, June 5, 1825,' in *The Works of the Rev. Robert Hall, A. M.*, eds Olinthus Gregory and Joseph Belcher (New York: Harper & Brothers, 1854), I, 213–24. Later in the nineteenth century, James Culross devoted a significant section of his *The Three Rylands: A hundred years of various Christian service* (London: Elliot Stock, 1897) to recounting the life and ministry of John Ryland Jr (pages 69–91). An examination of Ryland's theology may be found in the excellent study by L. G. Champion 'The Theology of John Ryland: Its Sources and

Influences,' *The Baptist Quarterly*, 28 (1979–1980), 17–29.

14. John Ryland, 'Autograph Reminiscences' (Ms. Z.f.31; Bristol College Library, Bristol College, Bristol), 44.

15. During his early years of ministry Ryland received much solid and judicious advice and encouragement from John Newton (1725–1807), the Anglican Evangelical. Ryland's friendship with Newton began a few years after the latter had become the curate at the parish church in Olney in 1764. It lasted until Newton's death in 1807. The year before Ryland's own death in 1825, he summed up his friendship with Newton in this way: 'Mr. Newton invited me to visit him at Olney, in 1768; and from thence to his death, I always esteemed him, and Mr. [Robert] Hall [Sr.] of Arnsby … as my wisest and most faithful counsellors, in all difficulties.' ['Remarks on the Quarterly Review, for April 1824, Relative to the Memoirs of Scott and Newton' in his *Pastoral Memorials* (London: B. J. Holdsworth, 1828), II, 346]. For a discussion of the friendship between Ryland and Newton, see especially Grant Gordon, ed., *Wise Counsel: John Newton's Letters to John Ryland Jr* (Edinburgh/Carlisle, Pennsylvania: Banner of Truth, 2009). See also L. G. Champion, 'The Letters of John Newton to John Ryland', *The Baptist Quarterly*, 27 (1977–1978), 157–63; *idem*, 'Theology of John Ryland', 17–18, 26.

On the life and ministry of Robert Hall Sr, see Graham W. Hughes, 'Robert Hall of Arnesby: 1728–1791', *The Baptist Quarterly*, 10 (1940–1941), 444–7 and Michael A. G. Haykin, 'Robert Hall, Sr. (1728–1791)' in his ed., *The British Particular Baptists 1638-1910* (Springfield, Missouri: Particular Baptist Press, 1998), I, 203-211.

16. See Grant Gordon, 'The Call of Dr John Ryland Jr', *The Baptist Quarterly*, 34 (1991–1992), 214–27.

17. Letter to John Williams, 5 April 1816 (American Baptist Historical Society, Atlanta, Georgia).

18. William B. Sprague, *Visits to European Celebrities* (Boston: Gould and Lincoln, 1855), 63.

19. A. C. Underwood, *A History of the English Baptists* [London: The Baptist Union Publication Dept. (Kingsgate Press), 1947], 166.

20. *The Admission of Unbaptized Persons to the Lord's Supper Inconsistent with the New Testament* [*The Complete Works of the Rev. Andrew Fuller*, revised Joseph Belcher (1845 ed.; repr. Harrisonburg, Virignia: Sprinkle Publications, 1988), III, 508)]. Fuller did not name Ryland specifically in this passage, but it is clear that he is referring to him.

21. See the remarks at the beginning of the sermon: Ryland Jr, *Indwelling and Righteousness of Christ*, 1–2.

22. *Indwelling and Righteousness of Christ*, 36–7.

23. *Life and Death of the Rev. Andrew Fuller*, viii–ix.

24. For this now obsolete meaning of the word 'tedious', see *The Oxford English Dictionary*, s.v.

25. 'Laughing the Night Away', *Christianity Today*, 37, no.3 (8 March 1993), 15.

26. Ryland, *Indwelling and Righteousness of Christ*, 35.

27. Maurice Roberts, 'Christian Friendships' in his *The Thought of God*

Notes

(Edinburgh: The Banner of Truth Trust, 1993), 175.

28. On this subject, see B. R. White, 'Open and Closed Membership among English and Welsh Baptists', *The Baptist Quarterly*, 24 (1971–1972), 330–4, 341; Walter Chantry, 'Communion: Open or Closed', *Baptist Reformation Review*, 6, No.4 (Winter 1977), 15–21; Joshua Thompson, 'The Communion Controversy and Irish Baptists', *Irish Baptist Historical Society Journal*, 20 (1987–1988), 26–35; Roland Burrows, 'The Closed Table ... Were Our Forefathers Wrong?', *Evangel*, 12, No.1 (Spring 1994), 23–28.

29. For Fuller's views, see *Thoughts on Open Communion* (1800) (*Works*, III, 503–6); *Strict Communion in the Mission Church at Serampore* (1814) (*Works*, III, 507); *The Admission of Unbaptized Persons to the Lord's Supper Inconsistent with the New Testament* (*Works*, III, 508–15).

30. Gordon, 'Call of Dr John Ryland', 217.

31. For what follows and the quotes, see E. Daniel Potts, "'I throw away the guns to preserve the ship": A Note on the Serampore Trio', *The Baptist Quarterly*, 20 (1963–1964), 115–17.

32. *Life and Death of the Rev. Andrew Fuller*, ix-x.

33. William Carey, Letter to John Ryland, 15 November 1815 [in Terry G. Carter, ed., *The Journal and Selected Letters of William Carey* (Macon, Georgia: Smyth & Helwys Publishing, 2000), 199].

34. *Life and Death of the Rev. Andrew Fuller*, 356.

35. *Indwelling and Righteousness of Christ*, 33.

36. Diary entry for 2 January 1759 [*The Deserted Village. The Diary of an Oxfordshire Rector: James Newton of Nuneham Courtenay 1736–86*, transcribed and ed. Gavin Hannah (Stroud, Gloucestershire/Dover, New Hampshire: Alan Sutton, 1992), 2].

Chapter 4

1. Comparatively little research has been done on the life or theology of John Sutcliff. There is a biographical sketch by Andrew Fuller attached to his funeral sermon for Sutcliff: *The Principles and Prospects of a Servant of Christ* [*The Complete Works of the Rev. Andrew Fuller*, revised Joseph Belcher (1845 ed.; repr. Harrisonburg, Virignia: Sprinkle Publications, 1988), I, 342–56]. Kenneth W. H. Howard, who was pastor of Sutcliff Baptist Church in Olney from 1949–54, has written a fine biographical piece: 'John Sutcliff of Olney', *The Baptist Quarterly*, 14 (1951–1952), 304–9. See also my *One heart and one soul: John Sutcliff of Olney, his friends, and his times* (Darlington, Co. Durham: Evangelical Press, 1994).

2. For Whitefield's influence on Fawcett, see [John Fawcett Jr], *An Account of the Life, Ministry, and Writings of the Late Rev. John Fawcett D.D.* (London: Baldwin, Cradock, and Joy/Halifax: P.K. Holden, 1818), 15–19. For that of Grimshaw on Fawcett, see Frank Baker, *William Grimshaw, 1708-1763* (London: The Epworth Press, 1963), 271. On Whitefield's influence on the Baptists in general, see especially Olin C. Robison, 'The Particular Baptists in England, 1760–1820' (Unpublished D. Phil. Thesis, Regent's Park College, Oxford University, 1963), 145–53; Raymond Brown, *The English Baptists of*

the Eighteenth Century (London: The Baptist Historical Society, 1986), 76–82; Deryck W. Lovegrove, *Established Church, Sectarian People. Itinerancy and the transformation of English Dissent, 1780-1830* (Cambridge: Cambridge University Press, 1988), 16, 69.

3. *Life, Ministry, and Writings of the Late Rev. John Fawcett*, 15.

4. 'Book Reviews: *America's Theologian: A Recommendation of Jonathan Edwards*. By Robert W. Jenson', *Church History*, 58 (1989), 522.

5. Extremely helpful in summarizing Edwards' thought in this paragraph has been David W. Kling, 'The New Divinity and the Origins of the American Board of Commissioners for Foreign Missions', *Church History*, 72 (2003), 799-807.

6. Susannah Spurgeon and J. W. Harrald, *C. H. Spurgeon's Autobiography* (London: Passmore and Alabaster, 1899), I, 310.

7. Fuller, *Principles and Prospects* (*Complete Works of the Rev. Andrew Fuller*, I, 350).

8. For an examination of ninety-one letters written to either Ryland or his father by Erskine, see Jonathan Yeager, 'The Letters of John Erskine to the Rylands', *Eusebeia: The Bulletin of The Andrew Fuller Center for Baptist Studies*, 9 (Spring 2008), 183-95. For the letter that accompanied the gift of Edwards' *Humble Attempt*, see Yeager, 'Letters of John Erskine to the Rylands', 187-8. When Erskine sent his copy of this book to the younger Rytland, he noted, 'I know not if there is another copy in Scotland' (187).

9. J. A. De Jong, *As the Waters Cover the Sea: Millennial Expectations in the Reformation today Rise of Anglo-America missions, 1640-1810* (Kampen, The Netherlands: J. H. Kok N.V., 1970), 166.

10. *Jonathan Edwards. A New Biography* (Edinburgh: The Banner of Truth Trust, 1987), 299.

11. *The Nature and Importance of Walking by Faith* (*Complete Works of the Rev. Andrew Fuller*, I, 117, note *).

12. *Nature and Importance of Walking by Faith* (*Complete Works of the Rev. Andrew Fuller*, I, 131).

13. 'The Prayer Call of 1784', attached to John Ryland Jr, *The Nature, Evidences, and Advantages, of Humility* (Circular Letter of the Northamptonshire Association, 1784), 12. For a detailed study of this influential call to prayer, see especially Ernest A. Payne, *The Prayer Call of 1784* (London: Baptist Laymen's Missionary Movement, 1941).

14. Ryland Jr, *Nature, Evidences, and Advantages of Humility*, 12.

15. *Jealousy for the Lord of Hosts Illustrated* (London: W. Button, 1791), 12.

16. Olney Church Book III, Sutcliff Baptist Church, Olney, Buckinghamshire, entry for 29 June 1784.

17. *Authority and Sanctification of the Lord's Day, Explained and Enforced* (Circular Letter of the Northamptonshire Association, 1786), 1-2.

18. Michael J. Crawford, *Seasons of Grace. Colonial New England's Revival Tradition in Its British Context* (New York: Oxford University Press, 1991), 229.

19. *Authority and Sanctification of the Lord's Day*, 2.

Notes

20. These would probably have been lengthy prayers.
21. Cited Jonathan Edwards, Ryland, 'Memoir of Dr. Ryland' in *Pastoral Memorials: Selected from the Manuscripts of the Late Revd. John Ryland, D.D. of Bristol* (London: B.J. Holdsworth, 1826), I, 17.
22. 'Preface' to Jonathan Edwards, *An Humble Attempt to Promote Explicit Agreement and Visible Union of God's People in Extraordinary Prayer, For the Revival of Religion and the Advancement of Christ's Kingdom on Earth, pursuant to Scripture-Promises and Prophecies concerning the Last Time* (1748 ed.; repr. Northampton: T. Dicey and Co., 1789), iv–vi.
23. For the details, see below chapter 7.
24. *The Baptist Annual Register*, 2 (London, 1797), 16, 23.
25. *The Baptist Annual Register*, 3 (London, 1801), 40, 42.
26. *Baptist Annual Register*, 3:40.
27. Lovegrove, *Established Church, Sectarian People*, 38.
28. *History of the Baptist Missionary Society, From 1792 to 1842* (London: T. Ward & Co./G. & J. Dyer, 1842), 1:10–11.
29. J. Edwin Orr, *The Eager Feet: Evangelical Awakenings 1790-1830* (Chicago: Moody Press, 1975), 95, 191–2, 199; Paul E. G. Cook, 'The Forgotten Revival' in *Preaching and Revival* (London: The Westminster Conference, 1984), 92.
30. Fuller, *Principles and Prospects* (*Complete Works of the Rev. Andrew Fuller*, I, 344).
31. Cited J. W. Morris, *Memoirs of the Life and Writings of the Rev. Andrew Fuller* (London, 1816), 443.

Chapter 5

1. On Fuller, see John Ryland Jr, *The Work of Faith, the Labour of Love, and the Patience of Hope Illustrated; in the Life and Death of the Reverend Andrew Fuller* (London: Button & Son, 1816). A second edition of this biography appeared in 1818. When Ryland's book has been referenced in this paper, it is the second edition that has been cited.

    For more recent studies, see Gilbert S. Laws, *Andrew Fuller: Pastor, Theologian, Ropeholder* (London: Carey Press, 1942); Phil Roberts, 'Andrew Fuller' in Timothy George and David S. Dockery, eds, *Baptist Theologians* (Nashville: Broadman Press, 1990), 121–39; Peter J. Morden, *Offering Christ to the World: Andrew Fuller (1754–1815) and the Revival of Eighteenth-Century Particular Baptist Life* (Carlisle, Cumbria, U.K./Waynesboro, Georgia: Paternoster Press, 2003); Michael A. G. Haykin, ed., *'At the Pure Fountain of Thy Word': Andrew Fuller as an Apologist* (Carlisle, Cumbria, U.K./Waynesboro, Georgia: Paternoster Press, 2004); Paul Brewster, *Andrew Fuller: Model Pastor-Theologian* (Nashville, Tennessee: Broadman & Holman, 2010).
2. 'Where Would We Be Without Staupitz?', *Christianity Today*, 35, No.15 (16 December 1991), 31.
3. Cited Laws, *Andrew Fuller*, 127.
4. Fuller's main refutation of Socinianism may be found in *The Calvinistic and Socinian Systems Examined and Compared, as to their Moral Tendency* [*The*

Complete Works of the Rev. Andrew Fuller, revised Joseph Belcher (1845 ed.; repr. Harrisonburg, Virginia: Sprinkle Publications, 1988), II, 108–242]. His chief response to Deism, especially that of the popularizer Thomas Paine (1737–1809), is *The Gospel Its Own Witness* (*Complete Works of the Rev. Andrew Fuller*, II, 1–107). For his reply to Sandemanianism, see *Strictures on Sandemanianism, in Twelve Letters to a Friend* (*Complete Works of the Rev. Andrew Fuller*, II, 561–646). For examinations of Fuller's reply to these and theological errors, see the various essays in Haykin, ed., '*At the Pure Fountain of Thy Word*'.

5. Andrew Fuller, Letter to William Carey, 18 April 1799 (The Letters of Andrew Fuller, typescript ms., Angus Library, Regent's Park College, Oxford University). I wish to thank Mr. A. Chadwick Mauldin of Fort Worth, Texas, for drawing my attention to this remark.
6. 'Andrew Fuller', 132–3.
7. Andrew Gunton Fuller, 'Memoir' (*Complete Works of the Rev. Andrew Fuller*, I, 1). For details of Fuller's family, see Ryland, *Life and Death of the Rev. Andrew Fuller*, 8–10; Andrew Gunton Fuller, *Andrew Fuller* (London: Hodder and Stoughton, 1882), 11–12.
8. [Ted Wilson], *Soham Baptist Church 250th Anniversary 1752–2002* ([Soham]: [Soham Baptist Church], 2002), [1]. This is an eight-page stapled pamphlet without pagination.
9. L. G. Champion, L. E. Addicott, and K. A. C. Parsons, *Church Book: St Andrew's Street Baptist Church, Cambridge 1720–1832* (London: Baptist Historical Society, 1991), 17.
10. Fuller, 'Memoir' (*Complete Works of the Rev. Andrew Fuller*, I, 2, 12). Also see Michael A. G. Haykin, *The Armies of the Lamb: The spirituality of Andrew Fuller* (Dundas, Ontario: Joshua Press, 2001), 59. For an overview of the history of Hyper-Calvinism in this period, see Peter Toon, *The Emergence of Hyper-Calvinism in English Nonconformity, 1689–1765* (London: Olive Tree, 1967).
11. Fuller, 'Memoir' (*Complete Works of the Rev. Andrew Fuller*, I, 2).
12. Fuller, 'Memoir' (*Complete Works of the Rev. Andrew Fuller*, I, 2).
13. Haykin, *Armies of the Lamb*, 62–3.
14. Haykin, *Armies of the Lamb*, 63–4.
15. Haykin, *Armies of the Lamb*, 69–71.
16. Andrew Fuller, *Strictures on Sandemanianism, in Twelve Letters to a Friend* (*Complete Works of the Rev. Andrew Fuller*, II, 563–4). See also E. F. Clipsham, 'Andrew Fuller and Fullerism: A Study in Evangelical Calvinism', *The Baptist Quarterly*, 20 (1963–1964), 103.
17. Haykin, *Armies of the Lamb*, 71–2.
18. Clipsham, 'Andrew Fuller and Fullerism', 106–7.
19. Fuller compared his movement out of Hyper-Calvinism to the finding of a path out of a labyrinth: Fuller, 'Memoir' (*Complete Works of the Rev. Andrew Fuller*, I, 13).
20. Fuller, 'Memoir' (*Complete Works of the Rev. Andrew Fuller*, I, 12).
21. Fuller, 'Memoir' (*Complete Works of the Rev. Andrew Fuller*, I, 15).

Notes

22. Fuller, 'Memoir' (*Complete Works of the Rev. Andrew Fuller*, I, 23).
23. Fuller, 'Memoir' (*Complete Works of the Rev. Andrew Fuller*, I, 25), Diary entries for 5 and 8 February 1781.
24. *Confession of Faith* XV in Haykin, ed., *Armies of the Lamb*, 279.
25. 'Northamptonshire and *The Modern Question*: A Turning-point in Eighteenth-Century Dissent' in his *Studies in English Dissent* (Weston Rhyn, Oswestry, Shropshire: Quinta Press, 2002), 205.
26. 'Preface' to *The Gospel of Christ Worthy of All Acceptation* (1st ed.; Northampton, [1785]), iv. Subsequent references to this work are to the first edition unless otherwise noted.
27. For the second edition, see *Complete Works of the Rev. Andrew Fuller*, II, 328–416. For studies of this work, see Clipsham, 'Andrew Fuller and Fullerism', 214–25; Morden, *Offering Christ to the World*, 23–76.
28. *The Gospel Worthy of All Acceptation* (*Complete Works of the Rev. Andrew Fuller*, II, 343). Extremely helpful in tracing the differences between the two editions is Robert W. Oliver, *History of the English Calvinistic Baptists 1771-1892: From John Gill to C.H. Spurgeon* (Edinburgh/Carlisle: Banner of Truth, 2006), 156–72.
29. 'Preface' to *Gospel of Christ Worthy of All Acceptation*, iv.
30. *Gospel of Christ Worthy of All Acceptation*, 37.
31. 'Preface' to *Gospel of Christ Worthy of All Acceptation*, iii.
32. *Gospel of Christ Worthy of All Acceptation*, 37–9.
33. *Gospel of Christ Worthy of All Acceptation*, 40.
34. *Gospel of Christ Worthy of All Acceptation*, 40.
35. *Gospel of Christ Worthy of All Acceptation*, 40–3.
36. *Gospel of Christ Worthy of All Acceptation*, 43–4.
37. *Gospel of Christ Worthy of All Acceptation*, 163–72.
38. *Gospel Worthy of All Acceptation* (*Complete Works of the Rev. Andrew Fuller*, II, 387).
39. *Gospel Worthy of All Acceptation* (*Complete Works of the Rev. Andrew Fuller*, II, 387–93).
40. In Harry Boer's words: 'Fuller's insistence on the duty of all men everywhere to believe the gospel … played a determinative role in the crystallization of Carey's missionary vision' [*Pentecost and Missions* (Grand Rapids: Wm. B. Eerdmans, 1961), 24]. See also Brian Stanley, *The History of the Baptist Missionary Society 1792-1992* (Edinburgh: T&T Clark, 1992), 12–13.
41. 'Fullerism as opposed to Calvinism: A Historical and Theological Comparison of the Missiology of Andrew Fuller and John Calvin' (Unpublished M.A. thesis. Southwestern Baptist Theological Seminary, 2010), 79.
42. For what follows in this section on village preaching I am deeply indebted to Paul Brewster, 'Village Preaching and the Revival of English Particular Baptists in the late 18th Century' (Unpublished paper, 2006).
43. Andrew Fuller, *Diary* (Bristol Baptist College Archives, Bristol, England), 17 April 1784, to 16 December 1784.
44. Ryland, *Life and Death of the Rev. Andrew Fuller*, 115.
45. Ryland, *Life and Death of the Rev. Andrew Fuller*, 117–8.

46. *The Promise of the Spirit, the Grand Encouragement in Promoting the Gospel* (*Complete Works of the Rev. Andrew Fuller*, III, 359).

47. On Fuller's trips to Scotland, see Dudley Reeves, 'Andrew Fuller in Scotland', *The Banner of Truth*, 106–107 (July/August 1972), 33–40.

48. Doyle L. Young, 'Andrew Fuller and the Modern Mission Movement', *Baptist History and Heritage*, 17 (1982), 17–27.

49. Letter to John Ryland Jr, 25 May 1801 [cited Geoffrey F. Nuttall, 'Letters from Robert Hall to John Ryland 1791-1824', *The Baptist Quarterly*, 34 (1991–1992), 127].

50. See in this regard, Michael A. G. Haykin, '"Hazarding all for God at a clap": The Spirituality of Baptism among British Calvinistic Baptists', *The Baptist Quarterly*, 38 (1999–2000), 185–95.

51. *The Pastor's Address to his Christian Hearers, Entreating their Assistance in Promoting the Interest of Christ* (*Complete Works of the Rev. Andrew Fuller*, 346).

52. *Promise of the Spirit* (*Complete Works of the Rev. Andrew Fuller*, III, 359).

53. For these numbers, see J. H. Y. Briggs, *The English Baptists of the Nineteenth Century* (*A History of the English Baptists*, vol. 3 (Oxford: The Baptist Historical Society, 1994), 248–61.

54. The following extracts from the letters of Andrew Fuller are all cited by Doyle L. Young, 'The Place of Andrew Fuller in the Developing Modern Missions Movement' (Unpublished Ph. D. Thesis, Southwestern Baptist Theological Seminary, 1981), 232.

55. See Haykin, *Armies of the Lamb*, 97–8.

Chapter 6

1. *The Autobiography of William Jay*, eds George Redford and John Angell James (1854 ed.; repr. Edinburgh: The Banner of Truth Trust, 1974), 372–3.

2. *The History of Dissenters* (2nd ed.; London: Frederick Westley and A. H. Davis, 1833), II, 653.

3. See, for example, *The Life and Letters of John Angell James*, ed. R. W. Dale (3rd ed.; London: James Nisbet and Co., 1861), 67; John Angell James, *An Earnest Ministry the Want of the Times* (4th ed.; London: Hamilton, Adams, & Co., 1848), 272. The phrase appears to have originated with Pearce's friend, John Ryland Jr: see Ernest A. Payne, 'Samuel Pearce' in his *The First Generation: Early Leaders of the Baptist Missionary Society in England and America* (London: Carey Press, [1936]), 46.

4. 'Memoir of the Late Rev. Samuel Pearce, A.M.', *The Evangelical Magazine*, 8 (1800), 177.

5. Payne, 'Samuel Pearce', 47.

6. On Cheare, see Joseph Ivimey, *A History of the English Baptists* (London, 1814), II, 103–16.

7. *Words in Season* (London: Nathan Brookes, 1668), 250.

8. Andrew Fuller, *Memoirs of the Late Rev. Samuel Pearce, A. M.* (2nd ed.; Clipstone: J. W. Morris, 1801), 1–2. Henceforth cited as *Memoirs of the Late Rev. Samuel Pearce* (2nd ed.).

Notes

9. For the life of Birt, see the memoir by his son: John Birt, 'Memoir of the Late Rev. Isaiah Birt', *The Baptist Magazine*, 30 (1838), 54–9, 107–16, 197–203.
10. Samuel Pearce, Letter to Isaiah Birt, 27 October 1782 [*The Evangelical Magazine*, 15 (1807), 111].
11. *Memoirs of the Late Rev. Samuel Pearce* (2nd ed.), 2–3.
12. On the life and ministry of Evans, see especially Norman S. Moon, 'Caleb Evans, Founder of the Bristol Education Society', *The Baptist Quarterly*, 24 (1971–1972), 175–90; Roger Hayden, *Continuity and Change: Evangelical Calvinism among eighteenth-century Baptist ministers trained at Bristol Academy, 1690–1791* (Milton under Wychwood, Chipping Norton, Oxfordshire: Nigel Lynn Publishing, 2006), 120–41. On Hall, see, in particular, John Greene, *Reminiscences of the Rev. Robert Hall, A.M.* (2nd. ed; London: Frederick Westley and A. H. Davis, 1834); G. W. Hughes, *Robert Hall (1764–1831)* (London: Independent Press Ltd., 1961); George J. Griffin, 'Robert Hall's Contribution to Early Baptist Missions', *Baptist History and Heritage*, 3, No.1 (January, 1968), 3–8, 42; Thomas R. McKibbens Jr, *The Forgotten Heritage: A Lineage of Great Baptist Preaching* (Macon, Georgia: Mercer University Press, 1986), 61–6.
13. On the life and ministry of Steadman, see Thomas Steadman, *Memoir of the Rev. William Steadman, D.D.* (London: Thomas Ward and Co., 1838).
14. S. Pearce Carey, *Samuel Pearce, M. A., The Baptist Brainerd* (3rd ed.; London: The Carey Press, n.d.), 93–4.
15. Carey, *Samuel Pearce*, 95.
16. Carey, *Samuel Pearce*, 48-49.
17. Carey, *Samuel Pearce*, 113; Arthur S. Langley, *Birmingham Baptists: Past and Present* (London: The Kingsgate Press, 1939), 34. Even after Pearce's death, his wife Sarah could rejoice in people joining the church who had been saved under her husband's ministry. See Andrew Fuller, 'Memoir of Mrs. Pearce' in his *Memoirs of the Late Rev. Samuel Pearce, A. M.* (Philadelphia: Amercian Sunday School Union, 1829), 160–1.
18. Carey, *Samuel Pearce*, 97–8.
19. Fuller, *Memoirs of the Late Rev. Samuel Pearce* (2nd ed.), 123–4, 140–1.
20. Payne, 'Samuel Pearce', 48–9.
21. Fuller, *Memoirs of the Late Rev. Samuel Pearce* (2nd ed.), 80–1.
22. *The Second London Confession of Faith* 11.1, 2.
23. *The Doctrine of Salvation by Free Grace Alone* (1795; repr. n.p.: New York Baptist Association, 1855), 2.
24. Her father was Joshua Hopkins (d. 1798), a grocer and a deacon in Alcester Baptist Church, Warwickshire, for close to thirty years. Her maternal grandfather was John Ash (1724–79), pastor of the Baptist cause in Pershore, Worcestershire, and a noteworthy Baptist minister of the eighteenth century.
25. Letter to Sarah Hopkins, 24 December 1790 (Pearce-Carey Correspondence 1790–1828, Angus Library, Regent's Park College, University of Oxford).
26. Letter to Sarah Hopkins, 26 November 1790 (Samuel Pearce Carey Collection–Pearce Family Letters, Angus Library, Regent's Park College, University of Oxford).

27. S. Pearce Carey, 'Love Letters of Samuel Pearce', *The Baptist Quarterly*, 8 (1936–1937), 96. In his biography of Pearce, Carey has a slightly different version of this quote. Carey appears to have 'modernized' the sentence for the biography; see Carey, *Samuel Pearce*, 122.

28. Letter to Sarah Pearce, 31 August 1795 (Samuel Pearce Mss., Angus Library, Regent's Park College, University of Oxford).

29. Letters to Sarah Pearce, 7 September 1795, and undated (Samuel Pearce Mss.).

30. Letter to Sarah Pearce, 24 June 1796 (Samuel Pearce Mss.).

31. Letter to Rebecca Harris, 29 March 1800 (Samuel Pearce Mss.).

32. Letter to Sarah Pearce, 14 June 1793 (Samuel Pearce Mss.).

33. Fuller, *Memoirs of the Late Rev. Samuel Pearce* (2nd. ed.), 140. For crucicentrism as a distinctive characteristic of eighteenth-century Evangelicalism, see David Bebbington, *Evangelicalism in Modern Britain. A History from the 1730s to the 1980s* (1989 ed.; Grand Rapids: Baker Book House, 1992), 14–17.

34. Letter to Sarah Pearce, 11 July 1792 (Samuel Pearce Mss.).

35. F. A. Cox, *History of the Baptist Missionary Society, from 1792 to 1842* (London: T. Ward & Co./G. J. Dyer, 1842), I, 52–3.

36. Payne, 'Samuel Pearce', 50.

37. Fuller, *Memoirs of the Late Rev. Samuel Pearce* (2nd ed.), 38.

38. Fuller, *Memoirs of the Late Rev. Samuel Pearce* (2nd ed.), 59. For the diary, see Fuller, *Memoirs of the Late Rev. Samuel Pearce* (2nd ed.), 39–57. For some lengthy extracts from the diary, see also Michael A. G. Haykin, 'Samuel Pearce, Extracts from a Diary: Calvinist Baptist Spirituality in the Eighteenth Century', *The Banner of Truth*, 279 (December 1986), 9–18.

39. Fuller, *Memoirs of the Late Rev. Samuel Pearce* (2nd ed.), 55.

40. Fuller, *Memoirs of the Late Rev. Samuel Pearce* (2nd ed.), 35.

41. Letter to William Carey, 27 March 1795 [*Missionary Correspondence: containing Extracts of Letters from the late Mr. Samuel Pearce, to the Missionaries in India, Between the Years 1794, and 1798; and from Mr. John Thomas, from 1798, to 1800* (London: T. Gardiner and Son, 1814), 26, 30–1].

42. See Ralph D. Winter, 'William Carey's Major Novelty' in J. T. K. Daniel and R. E. Hedlund, eds, *Carey's Obligation and India's Renaissance* (Serampore, West Bengal: Council of Serampore College, 1993), 136–7. The author was actually asked these questions after a presentation of Pearce's life and ministry in the mid-1990s.

43. Letter to William Carey, 8 September 1797 (*Missionary Correspondence*, 53–4).

44. Andrew Fuller, Letter to William Carey, 18 April 1799 (Letters of Andrew Fuller, typescript transcript, Angus Library, Regent's Park College, University of Oxford); William Ward, Letter to William Carey, October 1798 [cited S. Pearce Carey, *William Carey*, ed. Peter Masters (London: Wakeman Trust, 1993), 172]. In his memoirs of Pearce, Fuller wrote that Pearce's sermon was 'full of a holy unction, and seemed to breathe an apostolical ardour' [*Memoirs of the Late Rev. Samuel Pearce* (2nd ed.), 100].

45. Cited Samuel Stennett, *Memoirs of the Life of the Rev. William Ward* (2nd ed.; London: J. Haddon, 1825), 55–6. This Samuel Stennett is not to be confused

with the well-known London Baptist pastor, Dr Samuel Stennett (1727–95). This Stennett was a friend of William Ward and pastored in Dublin, Ireland, for a period of time. See A. Christopher Smith, 'William Ward, Radical Reform, and Missions in the 1790s', *American Baptist Quarterly*, 10, no.3 (September 1991), 240, n.1.

46. Stennett, *Life of the Rev. William Ward*, 55–6.
47. Letter from William Ward, 13 May 1799, cited 'Biographical Notices: The Rev. Samuel Pearce' in [John Taylor,] *Biographies. Northamptonshire* (Northampton: Taylor & Son, 1901), 12.
48. *Retrospect of a Long Life: From 1815 to 1883* (New York: D. Appleton and Co., 1883), 45.
49. *Motives to Gratitude* (Birmingham: James Belcher, 1798), 18–19.
50. Cited Carey, *Samuel Pearce*, 189.
51. Letters to Sarah Pearce, 20 April 1799 and 3 May 1799 (Angus Library).
52. Ernest A. Payne, 'Some Samuel Pearce Documents', *The Baptist Quarterly*, 18 (1959–1960), 31.
53. Fuller, *Memoirs of the Late Rev. Samuel Pearce* (2nd ed.), 141.
54. 'The dying words of dear Br^r Pearce to his wife' (Samuel Pearce Mss.).
55. Cited Carey, *Samuel Pearce*, 188.

Chapter 7

1. Portions of this chapter appeared first as 'The Life of William Carey', *The Evangelical Baptist*, 41, No. 1 (November 1993), 4–7, 9. Used by permission.
2. On Carey's life, the classic studies are those by his nephew and grandson: Eustace Carey, *Memoir of William Carey, D.D.* (London: Jackson and Walford, 1836) — henceforth cited as Carey, *Memoir of William Carey* — and S. Pearce Carey, *William Carey* (8th ed.; London: The Carey Press, 1934) — henceforth cited as Carey, *William Carey*. Other important studies include George Smith, *The Life of William Carey: Shoemaker & Missionary* (London: J. M. Dent & Sons/New York: E. P. Dutton, 1909); Mary Drewery, *William Carey: Shoemaker and Missionary* (London: Hodder and Stoughton, 1978); Timothy George, *Faithful Witness: The Life and Mission of William Carey* (Leicester, England: Inter-Varsity Press, 1991) — a front cover blurb by J. I. Packer on this edition simply, but rightly, states, 'This is a book that will do us all good'; John Appleby, *'I Can Plod...' William Carey and the early years of the first Baptist missionary Society* (London: Grace Publications Trust, 2007).
3. *The Autobiography of William Jay*, eds. George Redford and John Angell James (1854 ed.; repr. Edinburgh: The Banner of Truth Trust, 1974), 275.
4. Cited Tom Hiney, *On the Missionary Trail* (London: Chatto & Windus, 2000), 222.
5. Letter to Jabez Carey, 17 May 1831 (Carey, *Memoir of William Carey*, 566–7).
6. A. Christopher Smith, 'The Legacy of William Carey', *International Bulletin of Missionary Research*, 16, No.1 (January 1992), 2.
7. Drewery, *William Carey*, 10.
8. Carey, *Memoir of William Carey*, 7.
9. Carey, *Memoir of William Carey*, 25.

10. Carey, *Memoir of William Carey*, 393.
11. Carey, *Memoir of William Carey*, 398.
12. For a recent study of Carey the botanist, see Keith Farrer, *William Carey: Missionary and Botanist* (Kew, Victoria, Australia: Carey Baptist Grammar School, 2005).
13. Carey, *Memoir of William Carey*, 12.
14. Carey, *Memoir of William Carey*, 12.
15. Carey, *Memoir of William Carey*, 14.
16. Carey, *Memoir of William Carey*, 12.
17. Drewery, *William Carey*, 23.
18. Carey, *Memoir of William Carey*, 16.
19. 'Divine Providence and Captain Cook', *The Banner of Truth*, 274 (July 1986), 7.
20. Carey, *Memoir of William Carey*, 18.
21. *An Enquiry into the Obligations of Christians, to Use Means for the Conversion of the Heathens* (1792 ed.; repr. Didcot, Oxfordshire: The Baptist Missionary Society, 1991), 40–1.
22. Carey, *Memoir of William Carey*, 32–3.
23. *The Christian Spirit which is essential to the triumph of the Kingdom of God* (London, 1824), 22–7.
24. John Newton (1725–1807) once described him as having 'many particularities which gave him an originality of character' [cited Josiah Bull, *John Newton of Olney and St. Mary Woolnoth. An Autobiography and Narrative* (London: The Religious Tract Society, 1868), 205].

    On Ryland, see William Newman, *Rylandiana: Reminiscences relating to the Rev. John Ryland, A. M. of Northampton* (London: George Wightman, 1835); James Culross, *The Three Rylands: A Hundred Years of Various Christian Service* (London: Elliot Stock, 1897), 9–66; Peter Naylor, 'John Collett Ryland (1723–92)' in Michael A. G. Haykin, ed., *The British Particular Baptists, 1638-1910* (Springfield, Missouri: Particular Baptist Press, 1998), I, 185–201; Robert W. Oliver, *History of the English Calvinistic Baptists 1771–1892: From John Gill to C. H. Spurgeon* (Edinburgh/Carlisle, Pennsylvania: The Banner of Truth Trust, 2006), 30–8. See also the sketch of Ryland's character by Jay, *Autobiography*, eds Redford and James, 286–96.
25. See, for example, Smith, *William Carey*, 23; F. Deaville Walker, *William Carey: Missionary Pioneer and Statesman* (1925 ed.; repr. Chicago: Moody Press, n.d.), 55, who attributes Ryland's remarks to 'ultra-Calvinistic theories'; Drewery, *William Carey*, 30–1; George, *Faithful Witness*, 54–5; Phillip R. Johnson, 'A Primer on Hyper-Calvinism' (1998; http://www.spurgeon. org/~phil/articles/hypercal.htm; accessed 10 February 2010); Malcolm B. Yarnell, III, *The Heart of A Baptist* (White Paper, No. 2; Fort Worth, Texas: The Center for Theological Research, Southwestern Baptist Theological Seminary, 2005), 2–3.
26. See Appleby, 'I Can Plod...', 61–3; Iain H. Murray, 'William Carey: Climbing the Rainbow', *The Banner of Truth*, 349 (October 1992), 20-1; Michael A. G. Haykin, 'John Collett Ryland & His Supposed Hyper-Calvinism Revisited'

Notes

(*Historia ecclesiastica*, 9 October 2007; http://www.andrewfullercenter.org/index.php/2007/10/jonh-collett-ryland-his-supposed-hyper-calvinism-revisited/; accessed 9 February 2010).

27. *Enquiry*, 8.
28. Cited J. E. Ryland, 'Memoir' in *Pastoral Memorials* (London: B.J. Holdsworth, 1826), I, 17, note.
29. David Kingdon, 'William Carey and the Origins of the Modern Missionary Movement' in *Fulfilling the Great Commission* (London: The Westminster Conference, 1992), 88.
30. See Zechariah 4:6.
31. *Enquiry*, 103–5.
32. See also Andrew F. Walls, 'Missionary Societies and the Fortunate Subversion of the Church', *The Evangelical Quarterly*, 60 (1988), 144.
33. *Enquiry*, 108.
34. On John Thomas, see Michael A. G. Haykin, *A Cloud of Witnesses: Calvinistic Baptists in the 18th Century* (ET Perspectives, No.3; Darlington, Evangelical Times, 2006), 52–8. For more detail, see also C. B. Lewis, *The Life of John Thomas* (London: Macmillan and Co., 1873). For a judicious assessment of Thomas' character, see also Andrew Fuller, 'Sketch of the Rev. John Thomas' in his *The Last Remains of the Rev. Andrew Fuller: Sermons, Essays, Letters, and Other Miscellaneous Papers, not included in his Published Works* (Philadelphia: American Baptist Publication Society, 1856), 322–7.
35. For Dorothy's story, see James R. Beck, *Dorothy Carey: The Tragic and Untold Story of Mrs. William Carey* (Grand Rapids: Baker Book House, 1992).
36. Cited E. Daniel Potts, *British Baptist Missionaries in India, 1793–1837* (Cambridge: University Press, 1967), 17.
37. Cited Pearce, *William Carey*, 268.
38. Lewis, *Life of John Thomas*, 368–9.
39. Smith, *William Carey*, 100.
40. Hiney, *On the Missionary Trail*, 21.
41. This is Smith's phrase for describing the translation work of Carey, *William Carey*, 175–200.
42. On Carey the translator, see Pearce, *William Carey*, 415–26.
43. Stephen Neill, *A History of Christianity in India 1707–1858* (Cambridge: Cambridge University Press, 1985), 190.
44. See, for example, 1 Peter 1:23; John 17:17; and Acts 20:32.
45. John Scott, *Letters and Papers of the Rev. Thomas Scott* (London: L. B. Seeley and Son, 1824), 254.
46. Letter to his sisters, 16 December 1831 (Carey, *Memoir of William Carey*, 568).

Conclusion

1. *Lectures on the Epistle of Paul the Apostle to the Romans* (New York: Robert Carter & Brothers, 1844), 76. These lectures were delivered from September 1819 to November 1823 in the parish of St. John's, Glasgow. I am indebted to Mr. Jason Fowler, the Archives and Special Collections Librarian at The

Southern Baptist Theological Seminary for this information.

2. On Fuller as an apologist, see Michael A. G. Haykin, ed., *'At the Pure Fountain of Thy Word': Andrew Fuller as an Apologist* (Carlisle, Cumbria, U.K./ Waynesboro, Georgia: Paternoster Press, 2004). Fuller and Chalmers knew and deeply respected one another. After a visit to Chalmers, for example, Fuller told him, 'I never think of my visit to you but with pleasure' [cited William Hanna, *Memoirs of the Life and Writings of Thomas Chalmers, D.D., LL.D.* (New York: Harper & Brothers, 1850), I, 341–2].

3. I.e. 'puff up'.

4. Ernest A. Payne, 'Some Sidelights on Pearce and His Friends', *The Baptist Quarterly*, 7 (1934–1935), 274–5. A modern rendering of 'puff off' is 'puff up'.

Appendix

1. This appendix originally appeared as a section of my booklet *Revivals and Signs and Wonders: Some Evangelical Perspectives from the Eighteenth Century* (Richmond Hill, Ontario: Canadian Christian Publications, 1994), 40–4, which has long been out of print.

2. See my '"Signs and Wonders": Some Evangelical Perspectives from the Eighteenth Century', *The Baptist Review of Theology*, 3, no.2 (Fall 1993), 4–27.

3. *The Necessity of the Trumpet's giving a certain Sound* (Bristol, 1813), 4.

4. 'The Design of Spiritual Gifts' in his *Pastoral Memorials: Selected from the Manuscripts of the Late Revd. John Ryland, D.D.* (London: B. J. Holdsworth, 1828), II, 67.

5. 'The Love of the Spirit' in his *Pastoral Memorials*, II, 42. See also Ryland's remarks in a sermon that he delivered in 1802 at the ordination of Thomas Morgan (1776-1857): *The Difficulties of the Christian Ministry, and the Means of surmournting them: with the Obedience of Churches to their Pastors explained and enforced* (Birmingham, 1802), 18–19.

6. Also see his 'The Desirableness of a Spiritual Taste' in his *Pastoral Memorials: Selected from the Manuscripts of the Late Revd. John Ryland, D.D.* (London: B. J. Holdsworth, 1826), I, 118; *idem*, 'Remarks on the Quarterly Review' in his *Pastoral Memorials*, II, 348; and *idem*, 'Remarks upon the Notion of Extraordinary Impulses and Impressions on the Imagination' in his *Pastoral Memorials*, II, 417–9.

7. Letter to Mary Carey, 14 December 1789 (Baptist Missionary Society Archives, Angus Library, Regent's Park College, Oxford). Used with permission. Some of the punctuation has been added to make this section of the letter read more easily.

8. *Godly Zeal, Described and Recommended* (Nottingham: 1792), 1–2, 15. See also Richard Lovelace, 'Baptism in the Holy Spirit and the Evangelical Tradition', *Pneuma*, 7 (1985), 115. On Ryland's pneumatology, see Michael Haykin, ' "The Sum of All Good": John Ryland Jr and the Doctrine of the Holy Spirit', *Churchman*, 103 (1989), 332–53.